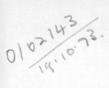

Boso's Life of
Alexander III

Boso's Life of Alexander III

Introduction by
PETER MUNZ

Translated by
G. M. ELLIS

OXFORD · BASIL BLACKWELL

ISBN 0 631 14990 2
Library of Congress Catalog Card Number: 72-96427

Printed in Great Britain by
Western Printing Services Ltd, Bristol

Introduction

Boso's history of Pope Alexander III (1159–1181) is the most remarkable part of the *Liber Pontificalis*. Unlike almost all the other contributions, it is far more than an informative chronicle. It is a work of history in its own right and falsely described as a Life of Alexander III. Boso's work is in fact a history of the long schism in the church brought about by the double election of 1159 and perpetuated until the Peace of Venice in 1177. It makes no claim to be a Life of Alexander because it not only says nothing about his career before his election but also purposely omits all those events and activities of his pontificate which do not strictly belong to the history of the schism. It ends with Alexander's return to Rome in 1176. Some historians have imagined that this ending was enforced by Boso's death which is supposed to have taken place in 1178.[1] But there is no need for such a supposition. The work, as it stands edited by Duchesne[2] and here translated, has a literary structure which reveals its purpose. There is a hero and a villain. The hero is Pope Alexander III, elected canonically to the See of St. Peter in 1159.[3] The

---

[1] H. K. Mann, *The Lives of the Popes in the Middle Ages*, London, 1925, Vol. X, p. 1.

[2] *Le Liber Pontificalis*, Paris, 1892; reprinted, 1955. Ch. H. Haskins, *The Renaissance of the 12th Century*, Meridian Books, 1957, p. 245 does less than justice to Boso when he says that 'Boso revives the fading tradition of the *Liber Pontificalis* by a revision of the earlier lives and by fuller biographies of the pontiffs of his own time'.

[3] The classical work on Alexander is H. Reuter, *Geschichte Alexanders III und der Kirche seiner Zeit*, 1st ed., 1845; 3 vols., 1860–4. There is a modern work on a smaller scale by M. W. Baldwin, *Alexander III and the 12th Century*, Glen Rock, N.J., 1968. The most authoritative account, though not biographical, is M. Pacaut, *Alexandre III*, Paris, 1956. The two older works, F. Loredano, *Vita di Alessandro Terzo, Pontefice Massimo*, Venice, 1637 and E. A. Brigidi, *Orlando Bandinelli, Alessandro III*, Siena, 1875, are now out of date, H. K. Mann's 'Alexandre III', *The Lives of the Popes*, London, 1925, X, is very informative but completely uncritical in its use of sources. J. Haller's portrait of Alexander, *Das Papsttum*, Stuttgart, 1952, Vol. III, is of lively interest though full of rash judgements.

villain is the Emperor Frederick I, surnamed Barbarossa (1152–1190).[4] In Boso's view Alexander had no other aim than to restore and preserve the unity of the Church; and Frederick had no other aim than to destroy that unity. But Alexander is presented in this story not just as an ordinary hero but the role he is said to have played is assimilated, quite explicitly, in one place to that of a mythical hero and we might leave further, more suggestive and specifically Christian comparison to the sensitive imagination of the reader. At the great cataclysm, when Rome was sacked in 1167 by Frederick's German warriors, Alexander, Boso tells us, suddenly disappeared from sight, but was seen three days later (sic!) 'dining with his companions (or ought we to read "disciples"?) at the foot of Monte Circello'.[5] And it is not without significance that Boso makes great play of the fact that after all his trials and humiliations, Alexander took formal possession of his earthly 'Kingdom', the City of Rome, on Easter Sunday. Alexander's long night of darkness ended with the return to Rome and his installation in the City was a form of political resurrection. It is not beyond the bounds of possibility that Boso in his pious imagination believed Alexander to be a Jesus figure.

The story of the contest between hero and villain[6] is so tersely and economically told that Boso makes no mention of the crucial role in the creation and perpetuation of the schism which contemporary opinion, with which Alexander is known to have concurred vociferously, attributed to Frederick's Chancellor, Rainald von Dassel.[7] The extraordinary omission of the famous or infamous Rainald is obviously dictated by dramatic purposes. If full account of Rainald's interest and of Frederick's reluctance were given, the drama would lose its simple confrontation structure. It would, in-

[4] For Frederick see P. Munz, *Frederick Barbarossa, A Study in Medieval Politics*, London, 1969 with full bibliography, pp. 401–410, hereafter quoted as FB.

[5] There was in fact sufficient doubt as to how exactly Alexander had managed to escape from Rome for Boso to leave his mythopoeic imagination free rein. Romuald of Salerno (MGH, *Scriptores*, Vol. 19, p. 436) said that he left the City disguised as a pilgrim and another annalist (MGH, *Scriptores*, Vol. 19, p. 285) reported that he sailed down the Tiber in a little boat.

[6] Although Boso's characterization of Alexander comes often close to the conventional traditions of hagiography, he is a little more circumspect in regard to Frederick. Boso never denies Frederick's intelligence, only his goodness.

[7] FB, p. 213, note 2.

deed, cease to be a drama and become a mere historical narrative. Are we to surmise that Boso had read his Aristotle and knew that poetry is superior to history? With this theory, Aristotle did not mean to extol poetic creativity in general at the expense of mindless recording, but meant to praise those writers who treated the epic traditions of Greece dramatically rather than prosaically.[8] Apart from the terse concentration on the clash between hero and villain, Boso's story has a genuine dramatic style. At only one single point, after the ratification of the Peace of Venice, does Boso lapse, strongly, into the conventional annalistic style and continues the next paragraph with the sentence: 'The nineteenth year of the Pontificate begins.' In view of the conception and composition of the work, one must assume that this stylistically inappropriate sentence is an editorial mistake, perpetrated inadvertently by a later editor or perhaps by Boso's own carelessness. This odd stylistic error apart, the composition preserves the full drama. It begins with an elaborate description of the confused circumstances surrounding the double election and then leads on to Alexander's plight as the victim of Frederick and Frederick's anti-Pope Victor IV. It ends with the elaborate description of the Peace of Venice in 1177 and the ceremonial pomp with which the reconciliation of Alexander and Frederick was consummated. The opening pages describe Alexander's flight from Rome and the concluding pages, his return to Rome. The events between the beginning and the end consist of a recital of the villain's stratagems, plots, conspiracies, aggressions, persecutions and injustices; and of Alexander's steadfast and determined manoeuvres to resist and defeat them. In order to underline the dramatic structure of the story, both the disaster at the beginning and the triumph at the end are supplemented—ought one to say symbolically supplemented?—by two circumstantial accounts of sea voyages. The first, surrounded by nautical hazards and perils, undertaken in flight from Frederick's persecution; the second, though not unaccompanied by storms and adventures, undertaken as a triumphal procession. On both occasions, in adversity as well as in triumph, the ships were supplied by Alexander's faithful patron and protector, the King of Sicily. The detailed description of Alexander's two sea voyages is neatly balanced by equally detailed descriptions of the villain's military defeats. The first occurred as the result of an epidemic in Rome in 1166 which reduced Frederick's armed might

[8] F. W. Walbank, 'History and Tragedy', *Historia*, 9, 1960.

3

to shambles. The second, equally detailed, but not half as truthful, is the account of Frederick's defeat near Alessandria. According to Boso, the city of Alessandria, named after his hero, was the great Lombard stronghold and the direct instrument of Frederick's complete military discomfiture in 1174. Boso's account of the foundation of the city and of Frederick's defeat at the hands of its citizens is untruthful and owes its remarkable presence to purely dramatic considerations.

Furthermore, the drama is not just the drama of the schism in the Church but of the schism seen in relation to the Pope's rule in the City of Rome. The story begins with the double election underlined by the fact that Alexander had to flee from Rome while his adversary Octavian managed to command the support of the City. The story ends not with the Peace of Venice which ended the schism, but with the return of Alexander to Rome—a return which was the direct military consequence of the end of the schism and Boso ends his story with the words 'he (Alexander) solemnly took possession of his kingdom' (i.e. Rome). In choosing the schism as his theme and in underpinning his choice with a definite interpretation of the direct consequences of the schism for the papacy (i.e. failure to maintain its secular rule in Rome) Boso not only displayed his sense of literary style but also showed that he had a very realistic and unsentimental understanding of 12th century ecclesiastical politics. Boso knew that the days had changed from the times when the Popes could claim to be rulers of Rome in virtue of the *status quo* supported or not supported by the Donation of Constantine. 'Indeed', he writes, 'the people (of Rome) have become quite unlike their forefathers in the days of St. Paul'. He does not hide the fact that the problem of the position of Alexander in the Church was intimately linked to the problem of his position in Rome. For instance, he gives a detailed account of the relations between Rome and Tusculum and discusses the eventual surrender of the latter very clearly as a question of whether the surrender was to be made to Rome or to the Papacy. Boso even makes out that Alexander had a special responsibility to the City ('that he could not in his fatherly kindness allow their backsliding . . .') and presents the situation as if papal secular rule had to be preserved in Rome for the sake of the City when the truth was all the time the other way round: papal secular rule over Rome had to be preserved for the benefit of the Papacy and the Church Universal. We can take the

4

fact that Boso interprets his chosen plot (the schism) in terms of Alexander's ability to maintain himself as the secular ruler of Rome as firm and reasoned evidence additional to the many separate and diverse pieces of evidence[9] we have for the progress of papal secular government and the territorial rounding off of papal secular rule during the second half of the twelfth century.

However this may be, the history which Boso writes has with its proper beginning and end all the hallmarks of a real story and, given Boso's concentration on a single theme and the dramatic structure of the work, it stands out among the other chronicles of the *Liber Pontificalis*.

When Muratori edited the *Liber Pontificalis* he attributed the work to Nicholas Roselli, the Cardinal of Aragon (d. 1362).[10] There is today, however, no doubt that the work was written by Boso and that it must be valued, therefore, as a contemporary account and in many parts as the report of an eye-witness. Unfortunately next to nothing is known about Boso.[11] He was an Englishman, the nephew of Nicholas Breakspear whom he accompanied to Rome. Nicholas, in 1155, was elected Pope Hadrian IV. Closely in touch with his uncle, Boso was made a Cardinal in the same year and became chamberlain, the most influential administrative official of the *curia*. As such he was in charge of papal finances and it is believed that he compiled the *Liber Censuum*. He was also put in charge of the Castle Sant' Angelo and employed as a legate to England. The office of papal chamberlain dates back to the pontificate of Urban II. In contrast to his predecessors whose main duty was the administration of papal revenues and properties, Boso made it his chief task to lay the foundations of papal territorial power in central Italy. He made some progress in this direction; but the success and continuation of his efforts were jeopardized during the long schism under Alexander III. It is therefore understandable that he gave some prominence to the precarious relations between Rome and Tusculum in his history of the schism, for the decline of the modest territorial advances made during the pontificate of Hadrian must have been a personal affront

[9] The sparse but telling existing evidence has been carefully sifted and presented in the first chapter of D. Waley, *The Papal State in the 13th Century*, London, 1961.

[10] His attribution was accepted by Migne, *Patrologia Latina*, Vol. CC, Paris, 1855.

[11] Cp. the attempt at a biography by F. Geisthard, *Der Kämmerer Boso*, Berlin, 1936.

and setback to Boso. Also, his interest in territorial aggrandizement gave his opposition to Frederick a very special edge. For the schism, if one takes a broader view, had resulted directly from the confrontation between Pope Hadrian and Frederick over territorial expansion in early 1159. Territorial consolidation of papal or imperial power was an issue on which Boso and Frederick must have understood each other. It just so happened that they stood on opposite sides of the fence. There can be no doubt that during Hadrian's pontificate he belonged to the small but influential group of Cardinals, led by Roland Bandinelli, who were responsible, in 1156, for the complete reversal of papal diplomacy which resulted in the alliance with King William of Sicily at the Treaty of Benevento and in the consequent deterioration of the relations with Emperor Frederick Barbarossa. The close connection between Roland Bandinelli and Boso survived the death of Hadrian in 1159 and until the time of his death in 1178 Boso remained a staunch and close friend of Roland who had become Pope Alexander III. Although Boso nowhere mentions himself or his role in the administration of the *curia*, there can be little doubt that he accompanied Alexander on his many journeys, some enforced and some voluntary, in the years of the schism and that in most parts his story is the story of an eye-witness. Needless to say, the dramatic conception that Alexander was the hero of the drama of the schism and Frederick its villain was suggested by Boso's personal sympathies and commitments.

In order to make Boso's story intelligible and a critical appreciation possible, it is necessary to place it in its setting. The middle of the 12th century was the end of an epoch. With the death of Bernard of Clairvaux in 1152 there had ended the enormous moral and personal influence he had wielded over several generations of Popes. Whatever opinion one may have of the salutary effects of that influence on papacy and Christendom, its success depended on the intentional absence of an institutional and legal frame-work. It was inspired by high-sounding moral and mystical aspirations, some of which were practical and beneficial extensions of the Gregorian Reform Movement; and others, fanatical and bigoted conceptions of the Christian religion which led to the persecution of Peter Abelard and the disastrous Second Crusade. The almost simultaneous deaths of Pope Eugene III (1153) and Bernard (1152) were the end of that epoch. Eugene, true to the spirit of Bernard, 'would have liked to arrest the papal descent into a vast ocean of litigation, but he had neither the knowledge nor the strength to do so. Among his successors Adrian IV accepted the situation with his habitual good humour and competence and Alexander III plunged into the intricacies of legal business with incomparable skill and zest. By the time of his death in 1181 the pattern of papal activity was fixed for the rest of the middle ages. It was not the pattern St. Bernard had desired. He wanted the pope to stand like Moses, in the words of Jethro, "for the people to go God-ward", "to teach them ordinances and laws and the way wherein they must walk", but not to judge between one man and another "in every small matter". But leadership could only be obtained on the terms that were available at the time. Leadership meant lordship, and the popes descended into the arena where lordship was to be won. It could only be won in the fashion of every other medieval ruler, in the ceaseless petty round of business and litigation.'[12]

After the brief and completely ineffectual pontificate of Anastasius IV (1153–1154), Nicholas Breakspear was elected and took the name of Hadrian IV. By that time, Roland Bandinelli was already firmly established at the *curia* and it is more than likely that he began to exercise a profound and leading influence on papal policy from the very beginning of Hadrian's pontificate.

Roland Bandinelli was born in Siena and spent the early years of his career in scholarly pursuits. He wrote a number of legal and philosophico-theological treatises and showed a great interest in the new systematic development of canon law, which found its first culmination in the work of Gratian. He had been a professor of canon law at Bologna at the time when Gratian in the same city was compiling his fundamental treatise, the *Decretum*. Roland himself wrote a *Summa* and *Sentences*[13]—books which brought him early fame as

[12] R. W. Southern, *Western Society and the Church in the Middle Ages*, Penguin Books, 1970, p. 111. Cp. also the following articles: F. J. Schmale, 'Papsttum und Kurie zwischen Gregor VII und Innocenz II', *Historische Zeitschrift*, 193, 1961; N. F. Cantor, 'The Crisis of Western Monasticism', *American Historical Review*, LXVI, 1960; H. V. White, 'The Gregorian Ideal and Saint Bernard of Clairvaux', *Journal of the History of Ideas*, XXI, 1960.

[13] A. M. Gietl, ed., *Die Sentenzen Rolands, nachmals Papstes Alexander III*, Freiburg i. Br., 1891. F. Thaner, ed., *Die Summa Magistri Rolandi nachmals Papstes Alexander III*, Innsbruck, 1874. H. Denifle, *Die Sentenzen Abelards*, pp. 424–434 believes in an early date for the composition of the *Sentences*, 1139–1141; M. Grabmann, *Die Geschichte der scholastischen Methode*, Freiburg, 1911, Vol. II, p. 225 agrees with Gietl, *op. cit.*, p. XVI on a much later date, possibly as late as the early fifties.

one of the most erudite and advanced thinkers of the age. They showed the influence of Peter Abelard both in the dialectical method of distinction and in much of the substance of his theological thought.[14] He was 'discovered' by Pope Eugene III in the autumn of 1148 and brought to Rome. In quick succession Magister Roland became Cardinal Deacon of Sts. Cosmas and Damian, Cardinal Priest of St. Mark and Chancellor of the Apostolic See. His intellectual brilliance was obviously matched by great diplomatic skill and political interests. Coming from a Siena middle-class background, he was wide open to the new developments in philosophy, theology and logic and his thought showed traces of calculating bourgeois intelligence. Apart from the influence of Abelard, his rational attempts to solve problems by distinguishing their components, places him with men like Nicholas of Amiens and William of Auxerre into the new philosophical current. In his legal reasoning he showed a marked distrust for historical precedent and a reliance on reason and equity and in his theology, a thoughtful rationalism rather than an adherence to the symbolic interpretations which still had a great vogue in the twelfth century.[15] As a practical

[14] D. E. Luscombe, *The School of Peter Abelard*, Cambridge, 1969, pp. 244–253. But cp. the review of this book by P. Munz, *The Journal of Religious History*, Vol. 6, 1971, pp. 286–90. F. Thaner, *Abelard und das Kanonische Recht*, Graz, 1900, p. 7, has shown that there is a complete identity between Gratian's and Abelard's dialectical method. Whatever the disagreements between Abelard and Roland were, there is no doubt that Roland stood firmly with Abelard on the side of the twelfth century rationalism which defined faith as an assessment of things that cannot be seen, half way between real knowledge and mere opinion. (Gietl, ed., *Sentences*, p. 11). In this matter Roland differed not only from such scholastic teachers as Hugh of St. Victor who defined faith as 'willing certainty' (*Patrologia Latina*, CLXXVI, 330) but also and even more from the long line of symbolic and mystical theologians who flourished in the twelfth century.

[15] Cp. the stimulating interpretation of Roland's thought in F. Heer, *Aufgang Europas*, Wien-Zürich, 1949, Ch. VIII. Heer is very inclined to see the whole dialectical and rational movement of twelfth century theology and law as a direct reflection of city life where people could not look upon their relations to each other in terms dictated by feudal hierarchy but had to forge them by equitable and pragmatic compromise between equals. This is a stimulating interpretation of Roland but it has, unfortunately, led Heer to see the whole clash between Frederick and Alexander in terms of the clash between the new bourgeois spirit and the old feudalism—the one anchored in the cities of Italy and France; the other, in the backward rural conditions of Germany. This interpretation of the conflict is very much at variance with the drama presented by Boso whose testimony Heer frequently quotes out of

man, he also had a sharp eye for the importance of administration and the building up of institutional frame-works. Here again, his early knowledge of the communal life of Siena, rudimentary as it was during the first half of the twelfth century, must have taught him the importance not only of law and systematic administration but also provided him with the humane background upon which communal life in the cities of Italy was founded. As a result he became one of the most active and enterprising canon lawyers of the medieval church and his legislation bears the stamp of that urbane humanity. When the Count of Flanders, to give a random example, had exiled a woman for seven years for the murder of her illegitimate son, she appealed to Alexander and offered a pilgrimage to Jerusalem as penance. Alexander replied that her presence in the Holy Land at this juncture would serve no useful purpose and decreed that she was either to enter a monastry or get married. Another woman who had strangled one of her many children was exiled by the lord of her manor. On appeal, Alexander decreed that, since her other children needed her attention, she was to undergo a different form of penance. Together with such practical humaneness,[16] Alexander also understood clearly that the Roman Church was the proper heir to the Roman Empire and that the Pope's universal aspirations ought to be translated into legislative and institutional practice.[17] In this respect, he went far beyond the somewhat woolly conceptions of Gregory VII about the primacy of *sacerdotium*, revolving as it did around a rough definition of simony. In short, without departing in any way from the general inspiration and guidance of the Gregorian Reform Movement, Alexander's practical experience and statesmanship

context. For a detailed criticism of Heer's interpretation of the twelfth Century see P. Munz, 'Frederick Barbarossa and the "Holy Empire"', *Journal of Religious History*, 3, 1964, pp. 20–25.

[16] W. Holtzmann, 'Die Register Alexanders III', *Quellen and Forschungen aus italienischen Archiven und Bibliotheken*, 30, 1940.

[17] G. Le Bras, 'Le droit romain au service de la domination pontificale', *Nouvelle revue historique de droit français et étranger*, 1949: Alexander, in all, issued 470 decretals. W. Holtzmann, 'Über eine Ausgabe der päpstlichen Dekretalen des 12. Jahrhunderts', *Nachrichten d.Akademie der Wissenschaften*, Göttingen, phil.-hist. Kl., 1945, p. 34 counts as many as 713. R. Southern, *op. cit.* p. 108–9, points out that the number of surviving papal letters, similarly, indicates a sharp rise in the volume of business. M. Pacaut, *op. cit.*, p. 260, points out that in absolute terms, i.e. taking into account the duration of the pontificates, Alexander's legislative activity was second only to that of Innocent III.

provided an institutional frame-work for it and translated the high-sounding phrases of Gregorian propaganda into administrative realities. One would have thought that the clash between Alexander and Frederick which brought about the long schism had its roots in these policies. And, indeed, there have been many historians who have been inclined to interpret the clash as yet another round in the long contest between empire and papacy for the primacy in Christendom. The irony of the matter is that during the pontificate of Alexander's predecessor Hadrian IV a number of letters and manifestoes about the theoretical questions of primacy were indeed exchanged. The debate turned on the question whether the empire was a papal fief and whether the pope was entitled to exercise jurisdiction over German bishops and whether the emperor owed his power to election by the German princes or to coronation by the Pope and whether the Pope was entitled, if he saw fit, to transfer the empire to the Greeks, and so forth. But all these debates took place during the years immediately following the coronation (1155) and before the final rupture in early 1159 and before the election of Alexander. They surround the ill-feeling caused on both sides by the diplomatic revolution enshrined in the Treaty of Benevento (1156) and it is noteworthy that on no occasion did any of these exchanges of theoretical opinion ever lead to a serious breach. In so far as they were not directly part of the cold war in the wake of diplomatic realignment of empire and papacy, they were part and parcel of the long drawn out movement which 'stripped the lay ruler of his supernatural pretensions'.[18] The movement was slow and gradual and stretched over the whole of the twelfth century. There were highlights in the debate; but there were no dramatic showdowns,[19] as

[18] R. W. Southern, *Western Society and the Church in the Middle Ages*, Penguin Books, 1970, p. 36. Southern points out that the 'thoughts on which royal government had acted for several centuries were blown away like airy nonsense. Almost no one bothered to defend them. The old sacred Kingship had no place in the world of business', *ibid.*, p. 37.

[19] W. Ullmann, 'The Pontificate of Adrian IV', *Cambridge Historical Journal*, XI, 1953, overdramatizes when he attributes the introduction of all the important changes in the imperial coronation ritual to Hadrian at the 1155 coronation. The changes which desacralized the coronation were very gradual and no one Pope can be credited with introducing them. Cp. E. Kantorowicz, *Laudes Regiae*, Berkeley and Los Angeles, 1958, p. 143. At any rate, a close examination of the circumstances of the 1155 coronation reveals that Hadrian was at that moment in no position to introduce any changes which might have annoyed or provoked Frederick. See FB, pp. 85–86.

Canossa (1077) had been. At any rate, the issues which had been raised in the wake of the diplomatic revolution had all been composed with mutual apologies by 1158 and when Alexander III became Pope, the clash became purely political and such debate of theoretical issues as there was, was kept at a very low key. The clash was certainly not caused by the debate. Frederick Barbarossa showed comparatively little interest[20] in this aspect of Roland's theocratic programme and if it had only been for this programme, there would, in all likelihood, never have been a clash, let alone a schism. Frederick started his career in the full determination to follow in the foot-steps of his predecessor, King Conrad III and to honour Conrad's promises to the papacy. This determination found its explicit statement in the Treaty of Constance between Frederick and Pope Eugene III in 1153.[21] And although the policy of the *curia* started

[20] Such interest as there was, was due almost entirely to Rainald, Frederick's Chancellor. See E. Otto, 'Frederick Barbarossa in Seinen Briefen', *Deutsches Archiv*. V, 1942. It is similarly clear from Rahewin's account of the famous Besançon incident in 1157 (*Gesta Frederici*, III, viii–x) that Rainald was much more interested in the theoretical issue than Frederick. Boso himself attributed no great importance to the theoretical issue raised by Rainald, as is proved by the fact that he completely omits Rainald from his story. On Alexander's side, an attempt to interpret the schism in wider theological terms is due to John of Salisbury. He argued that the supporters of Victor and Frederick are the party of the children of the world (= Augustine's citizens of the city of the Devil?) and quotes Jeremiah, xvii, 4 and John, x, i to describe the worldliness of the schismatics. W. J. Millor, H. E. Butler and C. N. L. Brooke eds., *The Letters of John of Salisbury*, London, 1955 No. 124, p. 208 and p. 214. As the editors comment, the second of these two passages bears great resemblance to St. Bernard's description of the 1130 schism. If, as the editors suggest, it was in fact derived from it, this would prove that John of Salisbury was not here paying much attention to the political peculiarities of the 1159 schism but was writing with a general rhetoric about schisms in mind. His views are, therefore, a *topos* rather than a reasoned theory. It is worth noting that Gerhoh of Reichersberg, a German publicist comparable to John of Salisbury, resisted the temptation to draw parallels between earlier schisms and the present schism. He disapproved equally of Victor and Alexander and blamed the schism on the material greed of the Roman Church. It is possible that his major work *The Search for the Antichrist*, was written in response to a request from Archbishop Eberhard of Salzburg who, on Alexander's side, was very disturbed by the schism. But Gerhoh's work is a major theologico-historical treatise. It far transcends all practical preoccupations with the immediate problems of the schism and belongs to the 12th Century literature of the symbolical interpretation of history.

[21] See FB, pp. 64 ff. For the history of the text of this Treaty see P. Munz,

to change during the pontificate of Hadrian IV, neither Frederick nor Hadrian wavered from the terms of this Treaty which was even officially confirmed in 1155.[22] Under the terms of this Treaty, Frederick promised help to the Pope against both the recalcitrant citizens of Rome and the aggressive policies of the Norman Kings of Sicily. And under the terms of this Treaty, Frederick came to Rome in 1155 and was crowned Emperor by Hadrian. Immediately after the coronation in Rome in 1155 it became clear, however, that Frederick was not able to fulfil his part of the bargain. He remained powerless against the citizens of Rome who opposed Hadrian; and his German princes and bishops who had accompanied him to Rome to be crowned, refused to embark upon a military expedition against the Normans in southern Italy. It was at this moment that Cardinal Roland seized his opportunity and won Hadrian's, though by no means the majority of the Cardinals', support for the diplomatic revolution which was consummated in the Treaty of Benevento of 1156, an alliance with the King of Sicily.

Frederick, cool statesman that he was, drew his own conclusions both from his failure to honour the terms of the Treaty of Constance and from the diplomatic revolution caused by the Treaty of Benevento and initiated a complete reversal of his own plans. He conceived a new plan to build up a central European Kingdom comprising Swabia, Burgundy and Lombardy and decided to leave the rest of the German princes as well as the problems of the Church Universal well alone. In the years following the reversal of alliances there were frictions between Empire and Papacy. But both sides took care not to go to the brink. There was no final rupture until the very beginning of 1159 when it became clear to Hadrian and Cardinal Roland that Frederick's new plan would lead to the incorporation of Lombardy in the central European Kingdom. And when Frederick scored decided, albeit temporary, successes in Lombardy towards the end of 1158, Hadrian with Roland's full support, decided on a final rupture. But this rupture was demonstrably due to conflicting territorial aspirations in Italy and had nothing to do with the larger, theoretical and speculative conflict between empire and papacy, between secular and spiritual power.[23]

'Why did Rahewin stop writing the Gesta Frederici?', *English Historical Review*, LXXXIV, 1969, p. 776.

[22] Cp. P. Rassow, *Honor Imperii*, new ed., München, 1961, pp. 66–7.
[23] FB, pp. 199f.

Even so, it is clear from Frederick's behaviour, that he would have preferred to contain the conflict and confine the rupture to the local, territorial dispute in northern and central Italy. But circumstances were against him. Because of the complete diplomatic rupture, Frederick had entered into relations with the citizens of Rome. Embassies had been exchanged and by the middle of 1159, just before Hadrian's untimely death, one of Frederick's military commanders, Otto von Wittelsbach, had taken up residence in Rome.[24]

Ever since the middle of the previous century, the relations between the citizens of Rome and the Popes had been precarious and strained. The leading Roman Families considered the Pope their ruler and had been accustomed for over three centuries to consider the rulership as the greatest political prize to be fought over and won by one or the other faction. With the advent of the Gregorian Reform Movement and the attempt to establish canonical rules for the orderly ecclesiastical election of Popes in the middle of the 11th century, the ascendancy of these various Roman factions was seriously threatened. For the Popes remained to all intents and purposes rulers of Rome; but were now to be elected not by the fighting factions of the leading families but by the Cardinals according to considerations that concerned the Church Universal. The Roman families felt thus deprived of the prize. Understandably, they also felt cheated of what they considered to be self-government and, last but not least, the removal of the election from competing parties, deprived Rome of cohesion. For there is a certain peace in the feud when the competing parties seek to capture one and the same prize.[25] The prize removed, the factions tend to become centrifugal. Moreover, the Popes elected by the Cardinals in the interests or alleged interests of the Church Universal were, more often than not, foreigners in Rome and had no faction to fall back upon for support in city politics. The Roman families themselves, in order to counteract the centrifugal force combined to set up a 'senate' in direct opposition to the alien popes which the Church Universal, through its Cardinals, kept foisting on them. For this reason, from the early 40's of the twelfth century onwards, the Popes had been living at daggers drawn with the citizens

24 FB, p. 205, and W. Holtzmann, 'Quellen und Forschungen zur Geschichte Friedrich Barbarossas', *Neues Archiv*, 48, 1930, p. 397.

25 Cp. The important theory of M. Gluckman, *Custom and Conflict in Africa*, Oxford, 1956, Ch. I.

B

of Rome and had frequently been forced to seek safety in exile from the city.

Hadrian himself had been forced to spend the last years of his life in Anagni and had died there in September 1159. At that time Otto von Wittelsbach and his armed men were firmly ensconced in Rome. The Cardinals decided that they ought to repair to Rome to bury Hadrian and elect a successor. But given the hostility of the Romans and the presence of Otto, a fighting man devoid of diplomatic finesse and political understanding, this was a hazardous undertaking. When the election finally took place, it turned out that a majority of Cardinals gave their vote to Roland, without doubt the ablest candidate and the candidate most likely to continue Hadrian's policies and preserve continuity. There was, however, another candidate, a friend and distant relative of Emperor Frederick. He clearly was unable to command a majority vote of the Cardinals. But he had close connections in Rome[26] and Otto von Wittelsbach, in his dim understanding of the situation, reasoned that if there was a contest it would be more advantageous to promote the succession of a friend of Frederick than of an enemy of Frederick. In this way, with the opportune help of a popular tumult and a little interference with armed force provided by Otto, Octavian was elected Pope Victor IV more or less by popular acclamation while Roland Bandinelli became Pope Alexander III through the majority vote of the Cardinals.

We shall never know the precise details of this double election. As was to be expected, both parties immediately embarked upon propaganda campaigns and the flood of letters and pamphlets which were poured over Christendom during the following fifteen years helped to erase much knowledge of what precisely happened and the allegations and counter-allegations laid a thick fog over the memory of contemporaries, and made the task of future historians hopelessly difficult. But the general outlines are clear enough. At that time Frederick was becoming more and more involved in the growing resistance to his plans in Lombardy. The last thing he could have wanted was a contested election and the endless complications it was bound to cause, complications which would effect not only his relations with the other Kings of Christendom but, more vital, his relations with his own Bishops on whose military support he now

---

[26] Cp. P. Kehr, 'Zur Geschichte Victors IV', *Neues Archiv*, 46, 1926 and H. Schwarzmaier, 'Zur Familie Viktors IV. in der Sabina', *Quellen und Forschungen aus italienischen Archiven und Bibliotheken*, 48, 1968.

depended more than ever as he was getting into deeper and deeper waters in Lombardy. Wisdom and foresight would have commanded him to throw his full support behind Alexander. But the temptation to support Victor was great, for Victor was a firm friend. In the days before the Gregorian Reform Movement, Victor would indeed have stood a good chance of success. But this was the middle of the twelfth century and Alexander had many powerful arguments up his sleeve which proved, given the climate of opinion, incontrovertible.

However this may be, the ensuing schism was neither planned by, nor advantageous to, Frederick. And this is the all-important point. For it shows that Boso's dramatic touch got the better of his judgement. Intent on writing a work of literature rather than a mere chronicle of the Life of Alexander, he had to have a villain as well as a hero. And thus he came to see the schism as a heresy engineered by Frederick in order to destroy the unity of the Church. Nothing was farther from the truth. Right from the beginning Frederick tried to heal the schism, though it must be admitted that when Alexander refused to attend the Council of Pavia in early 1160, where the disputed election was to be examined, Frederick all too eagerly gave way to the temptation to uphold the claims of Victor because he felt that, at least in the short run, it was the way of least resistance to have a friend and ally and distant relative on the papal throne. But this is all very different from the picture of a heretical villain whose single-minded purpose was to bring about the division of the Church.[27]

For that matter, Boso's picture of Alexander as the single-minded hero who had no thought other than to restore and preserve the unity of the Church Universal is equally dramatically distorted. It is, of course, perfectly true that Alexander wanted to end the schism by obtaining the obedience of the Church Universal. But he was by no means the innocent victim of Frederick's villainy to destroy the unity of the Church. Although Boso reveals none of this, Alexander's whole career from 1159 to 1176 was beset by difficulties caused by his own contradictory positions. These contradictory positions were

[27] Frederick far from being single-minded in his villainy was, like Alexander, very much a man of the new age. This is clearly borne out by Otto of Freising's *Gesta Frederici*. In Book I, Otto, sketched the background to Frederick's career and the two factors he thought most characteristic of the new age were the rise of the Staufen Family (I, viii–xiv) and the new philosophy (I, xlvii–lxi). He never defined the connection between the two in so many words. But the juxtaposition of the two accounts cannot have been accidental.

due neither to lack of understanding nor to any wilful or frivolous opportunism. Alexander had taken up, quite consciously the role of a politician when he left the schools of Bologna and joined the *curia*. It is unlikely that he could at that moment have foreseen the extraordinary political difficulties the papacy would have to face in the 60's and 70's. But we must always recall that he was a politician and that most of these contradictory attitudes were forced upon him by the political role he had to play. Deep down, and this runs right through Alexander's whole life, there was a basic inconsistency. He was influenced by Peter Abelard's new theology[28] and proved himself a dialectician of great skill in his own right. Roland was wide awake to the importance of the new school of thought. At the same time, he was firmly set against the growing 'heretical' movement and at the Council of Tours in 1163 he laid down the basic principles on which the Inquisition was later to be founded.[29] In this case, his attitude to new developments was discriminating. Just as he had not been a slavish but a discriminating disciple of Abelard, so he sought to discriminate between acceptable and non-acceptable trends in the new thought of the twelfth century. If this attitude was broadly ambiguous towards the novelties of the century, it was not downright inconsistent. Alexander's simple opposition to the heretical movement, however, was to have far-reaching consequences. He made no attempt to harness at least one wing of the heretical movement as Innocent III was to do in the case of the early Franciscans. Alexander's failure in this respect is all the more noteworthy since 'the first element in the success of the papacy in the eleventh and twelfth centuries was the support of religious communities who found in papal authority their best safeguard against the pressures of episcopal discipline and secular depredations'.[30] One might have thought that

[28] In spite of A. M. Gietl's conclusion that since Roland had differed so much from Abelard that he cannot be considered a pupil of Abelard (*op. cit.* p. xxx) D. E. Luscombe, *op. cit.* p. 253 points out that Roland even more than others was engaged in accommodating what was useful in Abelard's teaching and that the plan and method of his own work was Abelardian.

[29] Cp. G. Leff, *Heresy in the Later Middle Ages*, Manchester, 1967, vol. I, p. 36. H. Wolter, 'Das nachgregorianische Zeitalter' in H. Jedin ed., *Handbuch der Kirchengeschichte*, Freiburg, 1968, Vol. III, 2, p. 130, considers Alexander's step at Tours to have been more revolutionary than Leff allows.

[30] R. W. Southern, *op. cit.*, p. 127. Cp. H. Grundmann, *Religiöse Bewegungen im Mittelalter*, 2nd revised ed., 1961, p. 129 for Innocent's more politic attitude. See also sensitive appraisal of the intimate connections between

Alexander would have made some attempt at discrimination and taken a close and hard look at those 'heretics' who might have supported, if not papal sacerdotalism, the reform banner of apostolic poverty which Alexander himself decided to wave in order to win support against his imperial opponents. On a more immediately practical level, he declared himself a full sacerdotalist in theology and ecclesiastical administration.[31] But throughout the long years of his persecution by Frederick, he never hesitated to present himself to the world of Christendom as the *pauper Christi*, as a Jesus figure and as the very ideal of the growing spiritual movement which was agitating for apostolic poverty against the secular power of priests. His sacerdotalism and his opposition to the Roman commune had made him endorse the execution of the great leader of apostolic poverty, Arnold of Brescia. But his propaganda against Victor tried to make out that Victor was a heretic because he was rich and had wealthy patrons and was *not* a Christ figure, persecuted and poor.[32] It is not easy to determine the reasons for these inconsistencies. We know next to nothing about Alexander's personality. Boso is completely silent on the matter—a fact which further proves that the book in front of us is not a 'Life' of Alexander but a history of the schism. It is unlikely that Alexander was muddle-headed. It is more probable that these inconsistencies were due to the fact that he was thinker and politician at the same time and that these two different roles did not sit easily on him. His inconsistencies are indeed quite remarkable. Take, for instance, his attitude to Peter Lombard. Alexander's own theoretical writings, both the *Summa* and the *Sentences*, are both important parts of the newly developing dialectical rationalism which started with Abelard, was developed by Peter Lombard and found its fullest practice in St. Thomas Aquinas in the following century.[33] It so happened that for reasons which do not here concern us, Peter Lombard was strongly attacked by Joachim of Fiore and that the leading opponents of the new dialectical method,

the growth of heresy and the reformed papacy in the 11th century by R. I. Moore, 'The Origins of Medieval Heresy', *History*, 55, 1970. In fairness to Alexander one should recall, however, that at the Third Lateran Council, 1179, he did approve of Waldensian vows of poverty though he made their right to preach dependent on the local clergy's approval. Cp. G. Leff, *op. cit.* Vol. II, p. 448, and H. Grundmann, *op. cit.*, pp. 66, 98.

[31] Cp. the full discussion in M. Pacaut, *Alexandre III*, Paris, 1956.
[32] FB, pp. 220–1.
[33] M. Pacaut, *Alexandre III*, Paris, 1956, p. 73.

men like Richard of St. Victor, joined in this attack. This is understandable. But it is not equally understandable that Alexander at the Third Lateran Council in 1179 should have proposed to condemn Peter Lombard's *Sentences* as heretical. The condemnation was only avoided because Peter's faithful disciples rallied to his defence.[34] Alexander's attitude is even more incomprehensible when one recalls that Joachim's rejection of Peter Lombard's theory of the Trinity was based on the consideration that Peter Lombard's formula made the Trinity stand aloof from history and unable to enter into it—or so Joachim thought.[35] To Joachim 'the essence of the Trinity could not be thought of apart from its interpenetration of history: its unity in the divine sphere could only be expressed in terms of the "Three-are-One"; in the human sphere, by the unity of the *status* in history, developing towards one goal'.[36] Alexander's attempt to side with Joachim is all the more surprising when one recalls that Alexander, on many occasions, had expressed the belief that historical evolution, though undeniably having taken place, cannot give rise to rational arguments and that if there is a conflict between rational conclusions and historical evolution, then rational conclusions must prevail. In discussing, for example, the question whether it is sinful to purchase ecclesiastical benefices (simony), Roland unequivocally declared that it was sinful. Even Gratian had been less outspoken because he had been willing to take into account that the Prophets in the Old Testament had accepted 'presents'. Alexander brushed the historical precedent aside with the remark that bygones are bygones. Similarly, he insisted that the ancient practice of the marriage of priests and, under certain conditions, divorce, had existed in the primitive church but that that admission proved nothing. Times had changed and reason now commanded otherwise and reason must prevail over history.[37] With these views, one would have thought that Alexander would have had all sympathy with Peter Lombard and none with Joachim and that he was certain to side with Peter Lombard against Joachim's historicised theology. But he did not; and it is very hard to assess whether he had weighty intellectual reasons for not siding with Peter Lombard or whether at the Lateran Council in 1179 he took ecclesiastico-political considerations into account. Some light is shed on this question by Alexander's attitude

[34] M. Reeves, *The Influence of Prophecy in the Later Middle Ages*, Oxford 1969, p. 31.
[35] *Loc. cit.*   [36] *Loc. cit.*   [37] *Summa*, F. Thaner ed., p. 13.

to Gerhoh of Reichersberg. Gerhoh was a vociferous opponent of the new dialectical method in theology and in his *Book of Present-Day Novelties* very simply argued that newness was in itself worthy of condemnation. Alexander objected and wrote in 1164 both to Gerhoh and to his superior, the Archbishop of Salzburg, to suggest that Gerhoh keep silent.[38] Alexander's attitude here was completely consistent with his own theological method and his great interest in Abelard. But it so happened that Gerhoh had also doubted the canonicity of Alexander's election and believed that Alexander, like his opponent Octavian, had been guilty of simony because he had accepted money from the King of Sicily and possibly from other parties to ensure that, on Hadrian's death in 1159, a suitable successor would be elected, that is, a successor who could be counted on to continue the policy in opposition to Frederick which Hadrian had inaugurated during the last months of his pontificate. Alexander, therefore, had reasons other than purely intellectual ones for objecting to Gerhoh.[39] At the Council of Sens in 1164, in the very same year in which he had requested Gerhoh to keep silent, he supported Alan de Lille's argument that the new dialectical masters used a patently novel technical vocabulary and transgressed beyond the scriptural frontiers 'beyond which no citizen of the community of theologians is permitted to pass'.[40] Alexander roundly condemned at that Council the posing of 'undisciplined questions'.[41] Had he, at that moment, forgotten that he was the author of his own *Sentences* and of a *Summa*? At any rate, if his position at Sens was inconsistent with his own authorship of these works, his objection to Gerhoh's criticism of the theologians which Alexander himself criticized at Sens, was clearly dictated by political considerations, that is, by his dislike of Gerhoh's reservations about the canonicity of his, Alexander's, election to the Papal See.

Alexander's inconsistencies continued throughout his life on a more mundane level. Although Alexander made a great protestation

[38] Migne, *Patrologia Latina*, Vol. CC, Nos. 288–9.
[39] See note 43 below.
[40] *Summa*, Glorieux ed., p. 120.
[41] *Annales Reicherspergenses*, MGH, *Scriptores*, Vol. 17, p. 471. Cp. M.-D. Chenu, *Nature, Man and Society in the Twelfth Century*, Chicago and London, 1968, p. 323 and J. De Ghellinck, *Le mouvement théologique du XIIe siècle*, 1948, p. 252. P. Classen, *Gerhoch von Reichersberg*, Wiesbaden, 1960 p. 287–8, expressed some cautious scepticism in regard to the truth of the Reichersberg report since there exists no other source for this papal decision.

of Gregorian ideals and inveighed against simony, he constantly was in need of money and accepted money gifts in order to buy the favour of the Romans[42] and at least one perfectly honest churchman, Gerhoh of Reichersberg, at first refused his obedience to Alexander because he was sincerely convinced that Alexander was just as simoniacal as Victor, if not more.[43] And finally, on a purely political level, Alexander's position was gravely incoherent. Throughout the schism he gave his unstinting support to the Lombard towns who were resisting Frederick's suppression of their self-government and on many occasions he stiffened their resistance with special blessings and, at least on one occasion, with a wholly uncharitable piece of pontifical advice.[44] In some sense one might even say that had it not been for Alexander's astute political sense, Lombard resistance might have collapsed earlier and might never have been revived after 1165. For when Frederick caused most of the Bishops of Lombard cities to be deprived, Alexander, by skilful use of legates and by extending his right to appoint bishops, managed to gain full control over the ecclesiastical affairs of these cities and together with ecclesiastical affairs, over the communal administration.[45] And yet, at the same

[42] Boso himself is perfectly frank about the financial 'help' which Alexander was constantly obliged to seek and accept. On one touching occasion, he reports, Alexander was actually forced to forego a large sum of money which a Greek embassy had brought to Rome. In addition to the many instances mentioned by Boso, see also John of Salisbury, *Patrologia Latina*, CXXIX, No. 183 and *Policraticus*, VIII, 23 and Alexander's letter to a friend in Reims, Jaffé-Löwenfeld, *Regesta Pontificum Romanorum*, II, Leipzig, 1885–1888, No. 11256. There is also no doubt that on several occasions Alexander's support for Henry II was literally bought for money, Robertson and Sheppard eds., *Materials for the History of Thomas Becket*, London, 1875–85, Vol. V, Nos. 109–11 and Vol. VII, No. 751.

[43] *De Investigatione Antichristi*, MGH, *Libelli de Lite*, I, 55, p. 364 and 68, p. 385 and 69, p. 388. Gerhoh believed that Alexander was a simonist because when the Cardinals agreed at Anagni, prior to Hadrian's death, to elect Roland as his successor, they had received money from the King of Sicily to do so.

[44] On at least one occasion Alexander suggested that no more than the mildest of penances be exacted from a Milanese noble who had committed atrocities in fighting for the Lombard cause (= freedom of the Church) lest others be discouraged. See P. Kehr, *Italia Pontificia*, VI a, 36, note 187.

[45] G. Dunken, *Die politische Wirksamkeit der päpstlichen Legaten in der Zeit des Kampfes zwischen Kaisertum und Papsttum in Oberitalien unter Friedrich I*, Berlin, 1931; and W. Ohnsorge, *Die Legaten Alexanders III im ersten Jahrzehnt seines Pontifikats*, Berlin, 1928. See also FB, *op. cit.*, p. 281, note 3.

time when he was encouraging and propagating the communes' right to self-government, he completely failed to reach any understanding with the citizens of Rome who remained mostly, except for brief intervals when supplied with monetary bribes, hostile to Alexander, the self-proclaimed protagonist of civic liberties. A similar inconsistency is to be found on the international level. Alexander had been the chief architect of the alliance with the Norman Kings of Sicily. His whole career, throughout the schism, depended on this alliance as is amply made clear by Boso. Apart from Frederick himself, the Greek Emperor Manuel was the most bitter enemy of these Kings, for he considered them the tyrannous usurpers of southern Italy which had, until the arrival of the Normans in the second half of the eleventh century, been an integral part of the Byzantine Empire. But when Alexander was in dire straights and needed money and moral support, Manuel was willing to provide both. Alexander was caught in a cleft stick. Here he was, the great protagonist of the Church Universal and the unity of Christendom. How could he turn down the possibility of reunion with the Greeks which Manuel made a condition of his financial and moral support? And yet, how could he afford to alienate the Norman Kings of Sicily, who were equally munificent and whose moral support was so much more valuable because closely linked, in terms of geography, to the possibility of effective military and naval support? Not even Boso managed to gloss over this difficulty without comment.[46]

A similar ambiguity of attitude and policy is to be found in Alexander's treatment of Becket. Thomas Becket had condemned the Constitutions of Clarendon (1164) because they were incompatible with the new canon law propounded by Gratian. Many of the Constitutions had good old law on their side, but contradicted the new standards of episcopal and papal government in the Church.[47] One would have expected Alexander to side openly and clearly with Becket for he, like Becket, was a keen supporter of Gratian. But in fact, Alexander often temporized and often failed to give Becket his unstinting and unequivocal and consistent support.[48] Historians have

[46] See S. Runciman, *The Eastern Schism*, Oxford, 1955, pp. 120–1 and P. Lamma, *Comneni e Staufer*, Roma, 1955, Vol. II, pp. 195ff.

[47] F. Barlow, *The Feudal Kingdom of England*, London, 1961, p. 296..

[48] D. Knowles, *Thomas Becket*, London, pp. 104, 110–12. J. Haller, *Das Papsttum*, Stuttgart, 1952, III, p. 188. Haller, like so many other historians, sees nothing but weakness and ineptitude in Alexander's policy and is blind

varied slightly in their judgement of Alexander's motives for his
politic caution and prevarication. In broad outline, the reasons for
his caution are obvious enough. All through the 60's he was a fugitive himself and had to tread cautiously. But there is important
additional evidence to be gained from Boso's dramatization of Alexander's story. Becket 'studiously lifted the controversy on to the high
level of doctrinal and canonical theory, where it might meet and
mingle with the great Gregorian controversy of the preceding century'.[49] But to Boso—and we must presume, given the close friendship, also to Alexander—the high level was of little interest. Boso
presented the conflict between Alexander and Frederick as a conflict
between a villain and a hero. He made no attempt to present the
matter in doctrinal or canonical terms.[50] And as far as Alexander
was concerned, the Gregorian echoes were exploited more for purposes of propaganda than for anything else. At any rate if Boso
reflects Alexander's views, and we have every reason for believing
that he does, there was more than politic caution in Alexander's
restrained sympathy for Becket. Alexander simply found Becket's
studious attempt to lift the controversy to a high doctrinal level
unattractive and uninteresting as well as imprudent. His reluctance
to support Becket to the hilt was partially due to the fact that he
simply considered Becket's high-minded stance unrealistic and was
out of sympathy with it. Cowardice and caution may all have played
their part. But in fairness to Alexander Boso's testimony must not
be underrated. And Boso clearly saw the conflict between Alexander
and Frederick as a conflict between a villain and a hero, not as a
conflict over doctrinal matters. And it is highly likely that he did so
because the doctrinal aspects were of little interest to him. Hence it

to the political intricacy of the situation. Knowles is more sympathetic to
Alexander's quandary.

[49] D. Knowles, *The Episcopal Colleagues of Archbishop Thomas Becket*,
Cambridge, 1951, p. 150.

[50] Only in passing does Boso ever make reference to political doctrine. On
two incidental occasions he states that God has appointed two powers, Priest
and Emperor, for the government of Christendom and that these two powers
ought to be in unison. His formula is intentionally vague and only remotely
reminiscent of the Gelasian doctrine and the theory of the two swords. It
never stands out as a 'doctrine'. And if one is looking for a doctrine held by
Alexander it can hardly be found in Boso's vague statements, for as a programme for the papacy between Gregory VII and Innocent III, Boso's mild
formula was hardly suitable.

is reasonable to think that the doctrinal aspect of the parallel clash between Henry II and Becket, too, were of no great interest to him. Hence, in addition to Alexander's caution and prudence and perhaps even pusillanimity, there was a genuine disagreement between Alexander and Becket. Even so it remains true, however, that Alexander never made his position in this respect entirely clear to Becket. Perhaps if Becket had been able to read Boso's history of the schism, he would have gained a clearer understanding of the reasons for Alexander's lukewarm support. Becket did not know Boso's view of the situation and did not know of the Boso-Alexander self-dramatization. All he was acquainted with was the Gregorian propaganda and Alexander's protestation that he was the poor man of Christ and a fighter for the freedom of the Church. Taking this propaganda at its face-value, he had every reason to expect a complete identity of views and interests. Alexander's failure to identify himself wholeheartedly with Becket could not but be interpreted by historians as due to cowardice or politic caution. But if one considers Boso's and Alexander's real view of themselves as revealed in Boso's History, one will see that there were other reasons for this failure. One must conclude that there was a lack of communication between Alexander and Becket and attribute part of the tragedy to his lack. This is not to say that Alexander did not support Becket's stand and cause. But it does explain his lukewarmness and inconsistency. If Alexander had made himself clearer to Becket, the tragedy might not have occurred and one might even argue that Alexander, because of his failure to communicate to Becket how he and Boso saw themselves and the meaning of their fight against the schismatics and how they differed in their view of their fight from Becket's view of his fight against Henry II, bears a certain responsibility for the tragedy. For if Becket had been able to size up Alexander correctly he might, himself, have shown more moderation. According to Boso, Henry admitted, in the end, an indirect responsibility because of 'my troubled state and the anger which I conceived against the holy man'. He might have added that Alexander had a similar indirect responsibility because he had failed to let Becket know that he interpreted his stand against Frederick in terms that were completely different from the terms in which Becket saw his stand against Henry II and had allowed Becket to hope for more support than he was likely to get—a hope which from Becket's standpoint was not unjustified since he did not know Boso's view of

the fight as a drama and knew only of the identity of his protestations with the public declarations issued by Alexander.

However this may be, in this case as in many others, when political prudence commanded it, Alexander was quite prepared to make
wide concessions to territorial rulers' claims over the Church. There
is a considerable list of such concessions—a list which squares badly
with Alexander's theoretical pronouncements and public declarations.
Within a year of his election he made large concessions to the King
of Hungary.[51] In 1156, at the Treaty of Benevento, he supported
Hadrian's willingness to grant many ecclesiastical rights to the
Norman Kings of southern Italy.[52] At the Peace of Venice in 1177,
he was far from intransigent as far as the Empire was concerned.
Indeed, instead of insisting on Gregorian Reforms in the German
Church or at least of taking his stand on the Concordat of Worms
(1122), Alexander engaged with Frederick in a great deal of horse-
trading in regard to the German bishops.[53] And when the final
settlement with Henry II of England was agreed upon at Avranches
in 1172 we find again that Alexander thought it opportune to be
lenient. The terms of the agreement are quite favourable to Henry's
claims and when they became known, there were people who
thought that Becket's martyrdom had, after all, been in vain.[54] In

---

[51] W. Holtzmann, *Beiträge zur Reichs— und Rechtsgeschichte des hohen
Mittelalters*, Bonn, 1957, pp. 151–2.

[52] Thomas Becket described the Treaty roundly as a 'tyrannous usurpa-
tion', Bouquet, XVI, p. 300. For the ecclesiastical terms of the Treaty see
M. W. Baldwin, *Alexander III and the Twelfth Century*, Glen Rock, N.J.,
1968, p. 33.

[53] At Venice most of the agreements of Anagni, November 1176, were
confirmed. For the Anagni horse-trading see FB, *op. cit.*, p. 313.

[54] Cp. J. Haller, *op. cit.*, III, p. 221. Innocent III was of the opinion that
because of Avranches, Becket's martyrdom had been in vain, *Gesta, c.* 131.
For the terms of the agreement see M. W. Baldwin, *op. cit.*, p. 127 and D.
Knowles, *Thomas Becket*, London, 1970, p. 153. A detailed account of the
agreement is in D. C. Douglas and G. W. Greenaway, *English Historical
Documents* 1042–1189, London, 1953, pp. 773–4. For a realistic assessment
of the compromise of Avranches see H. Mayr-Harting, 'Henry II and the
Papacy, 1170–1189', *Journal of Ecclesiastical History*, 16, 1965, p. 48: 'The
King . . . made only one concession' and p. 53: 'Royal power was now
exercised completely by judicious interventions . . . but it was exercised
effectively for all that.'—In view of Boso's report that Henry abrogated all
'those unlawful customs which in my time I have introduced throughout
the length and breadth of my Kingdom' it is difficult to agree with D.
Knowles, *op. cit.*, p. 153, that there was no explicit renunciation of the

view of these widespread concessions, Boso thought it wise to include in his work the full text, although it does not fit into the story, of the final agreement with King Bela of Hungary. This final accommodation with Hungary was indeed in full accord with the principles for which Alexander had stood and for which he had declared himself to have been persecuted. But this accommodation was the only one in which these principles triumphed without question. Boso, therefore, included it, in spite of the dramatic inappropriateness, in full. Its full text was meant to prove that in spite of Avranches and Venice and Benevento and the earlier grants to Hungary, Alexander was, in the end, true to the new canon law and the Gregorian Reform.[55] In this matter, Boso must be excused. He knew that Alexander had often compromised for political reasons. But he knew that the compromises had been dictated by Alexander's steadfast wish to advance the cause of the new canon law and the Gregorian Reform. And so he thought it excusable to give, at the very end of his work, the impression that agreements of the kind which had been made with the King of Hungary were typical.

The dramatic structure of Boso's work is manifest. In some cases it led to downright distortion of the truth and in other cases it enabled him to narrate with a clear-sightedness which has since been corroborated by other documents. It is all too easy to dismiss a historian as unreliable as soon as one discovers that he is not a wholly impersonal collector of facts but that the conception of his work is based upon a literary structure. It would be ridiculous to

Constitutions of Clarendon. It is true that Boso does not mention them by name; but his reference is unmistakable. It is also true that at least on one specific point, Boso completely supports the conclusions reached by Z. N. Brooke, 'The Effect of Becket's Murder on Papal Authority in England', *Cambridge Historical Journal*, Vol. II, 1928, p. 225: 'The Pope . . . gained his end when he wrung from Henry after Becket's murder the concession allowing unrestricted appeals to Rome.' Brooke's conclusion is based entirely on a survey of papal decretals and therefore independently corroborates Boso's statement that Henry formally promised to 'allow appeals to the Apostolic See to be made freely'. Brooke's conclusion however, is not inconsistent with the opinions quoted above, for there were more matters involved than appeals to Rome.

[55] It is probably no accident that in the text as given by Boso, there should be a full and repeated clarification of the notorious problem of 'criminous clerks'.

compare Boso with Thucydides. But it is worth noting that Cornford's discovery of an underlying mythical pattern in Thucydides' conception of the history of the Peloponnesian War does not detract from Thucydides' stature as a historian.[56] Boso, like the incomparably greater Thucydides, has given us digested history rather than a mindless assortment of facts made slightly interesting by personal bias and an expression of prejudice. Boso's work, like Thucydides', has a structure. All the more important then to provide a brief indication of where other sources bear him out and where other sources have been found to contradict him.

First of all the examples which show Boso's truthfulness and reliability. There is no need to list every true sentence. Examination can be confined to those points where Boso showed himself truthful in spite of the fact that it did not really fit his preconceived drama. Boso, to start at the beginning of his story, was aware that Octavian, no matter how much of a heresiarch, had local Roman backing and that his initial success at the election has to be accounted for by his local support of members of his own family and their faction. Alexander was a foreigner in Rome. Octavian was not. Heresy and the desire to create schism may have entered into the situation, as Boso lost no time in pointing out. But Boso does not seek to conceal that Octavian was a 'local' man.[57] Another example of Boso's great truthfulness is provided by his account of the steps by which Alexander III was recognized by the Kings of France and England. According to Gerhoh who may either have been misinformed, confused or have had reasons of his own for painting a picture of the great joint manifestation of obedience to Alexander by the Kings of England and France, there was held a Council at Toulouse in the autumn of 1160 at which both Kings declared their obedience to Alexander.[58] Boso tells a very different story. He reports that Louis

[56] *Thucydides Mythistoricus*, London, 1907. Cp. also P. Munz, 'History and Myth', *Philosophical Quarterly*, 6, 1956.

[57] See above, note 26.

[58] The fact that Gerhoh, *De Investigatione Antichristi*, MGH, *Libelli de Lite*, III, p. 365, is the only source for the Council of Toulouse has made historians suspicious. Nevertheless a great many have accepted Gerhoh's story. For arguments in his favour and the relevant literature see P. Classen, *Gerhoch von Reichersberg*, Wiesbaden, 1960, p. 197, note 29. Whatever the merits of the arguments in favour of Gerhoh's story, they must lose much of their force when one considers Boso's silence about Toulouse. A joint demonstration by Henry and Louis for Alexander such as is alleged to have

VII of France recognized Alexander first in response to an embassy sent by Alexander on his arrival at Montpelier. Henry II of England, according to Boso, paid his personal respects and publicly demonstrated his obedience much later, when Alexander was residing at Déols. In fact, we know that there was actually more communication between the two Kings on this matter than Boso reveals even though it is highly unlikely that the concert was staged as solemnly as Gerhoh would have us believe. It would have suited Boso's story to make the most of this agreement of the two Kings. But he made very little of it because he bore in mind that Henry II and Louis VII rarely saw eye to eye and that any common demonstration in favour of Alexander was likely to be temporary and accidental and should not be viewed as proof of the concerted obedience of Christendom outside the confines of the empire.

In his account of the conspiracy with Henry of Troyes and the events leading to the meeting on the Saône, Boso is again completely right. Frederick, at this juncture, was determined to waylay Alexander and hatched a plan of the 'heads-I-win-tails-you-lose' kind. Boso gets some of the details wrong; but so do other writers and it has, therefore, been notoriously difficult to reconstruct with precision what took place. But in outline, Frederick planned to pack a Council. If Louis produced Alexander, the Council would find against him. If he did not produce him, Alexander was to forfeit the papacy automatically. Whichever way it went, Frederick could not lose.[59] There is ample evidence of the cunning manner in which he penned the letters of invitation to the proposed meeting.[60] Again, his account of the intolerable behaviour of Frederick's commissioners in Lombardy has found independent confirmation and we have no reason to doubt the truth of Boso's stories of oppression. He had cast Frederick as a villain; but it so happened that at least the results, if not the intentions, of his policies in Lombardy were indeed

taken place at Toulouse would have been grist to Boso's mill. The fact that he does not mention it must be taken as conclusive proof that Gerhoh's story is wrong. This conclusion fully vindicates F. Barlow, 'The English, Norman and French Councils called to deal with the Papal schism of 1159', *English Historical Review*, LI, 1936, and is given further strength by Mary G. Cheney, 'The Recognition of Pope Alexander III', *English Historical Review*, LXXXIV, 1969.

[59] Boso's story is corroborated by Hugh of Poitiers, MGH, *Scriptores*, 26, p. 147 and Saxo Grammaticus, MGH, *Scriptores*, 29, pp. 113–14.

[60] For these cunning invitations see FB, p. 229f.

villainous.[61] In 1167 when Frederick's army stormed and sacked Rome, Boso's account of the atrocities is fully borne out by independent sources.[62] On this occasion, Frederick again lived up to the role for which Boso had cast him. And when we turn to a minor matter, we find again that Boso was right. It has been suspected for some time that the city of Alessandria was not founded as a symbol of defiance against Frederick but that it became such a symbol when it turned out to have, accidentally, defied Frederick's assaults. Boso makes no bones about this. If Alessandria had been built as a stronghold against Frederick, it would have had proper walls and towers. Boso states that it had none. This bears out the view that it became a symbol of resistance as an afterthought and although Boso, true to his dramatic structure, seeks to present the fight in Lombardy as a fight for the unity of the Church, he is quite truthful in his description of the poor fortifications of Alessandria though not in his assessment of the role of that town.[63] He is similarly truthful about the popular rebellion against the consuls in Cremona. The consuls had been too friendly to Frederick on the occasion of his decision to abandon the fight against the Lombard League. The people disagreed with their rulers and deposed them. One might have thought that this story fits in too well with Boso's drama to be true. But it happens to *be* true.[64] The only point which Boso conceals is that the rebellion was probably instigated by the Bishop, an Alexander appointee. Boso is again truthful in his telescoping of the events which preceded the battle of Legnano. It would have suited his drama to relate in detail how Frederick begged the German princes for help and how they refused and one would have expected him to give particular emphasis to Henry the Lion's refusal to come to the succour of the excommunicated and desperate schismatic Frederick. But Boso makes no mention of Frederick's plight and of Henry's obdurate refusal. Subsequent research has shown that he was truth-

[61] FB, pp. 271ff.

[62] Helmold, *Chronica Slavorum* II, c.10; Otto of St. Blaise, c.20; *Weingarten Chronicle*, c. 32, 1167; *Chronicle of St. Peter at Erfurt*, 1166.

[63] Boso is in fact the only source for the story of Alessandria's festive and symbolic foundation. The other sources are to be found in H. Prutz, *Friedrich I*, 1870, vol. II, pp. 352–3. All the more credit to Boso for revealing the fact that, in spite of his own story, the founders of the city had failed to provide fortifications. The inconsistencies in the sources have been unravelled by F. Graf, *Die Gründung Alexandrias*, Berlin, 1887.

[64] F. Güterbock, *Der Friede von Montebello*, Berlin, 1895 and FB, p. 305.

ful and that other writers who have exploited the story and blown it up beyond all reasonable proportions, were not.[65] Skipping the battle of Legnano, we come to the Treaty of Anagni. Here again it would have fitted Boso's plot to present Frederick as a mere suppliant and Alexander as a gracious bestower of bounty. But Boso resisted the temptation to falsify to suit his drama. He does not quote the actual text of the Treaty; but the subsequent discovery of the Treaty has shown that Boso's summary of its provisions is substantially correct.[66] Coming next to the Peace of Venice, we find Boso's description of the position of the Lombard delegates to be truthful. It would have fitted in well with his drama to make the negotiations appear to have taken place between Alexander and Frederick's envoys. But Boso is truthful to a fault, for he quotes the Lombards' demands and we happen to know from Romuald of Salerno that the quotation is correct word for word[67] and that it was owing to these demands that it was not possible to achieve more than a seven-year truce with the Lombards at Venice. If Boso had wanted to stick blindly to the dramatic plot he had outlined for himself, it would have been easy for him not to quote these demands verbatim and to gloss them over. After the Peace of Venice, Alexander returned to Rome. Boso's plot would have required a story of triumph to seal the end of the schism and to make the most of the reconciliation between Romans and Alexander. But Boso was truthful. He tells us explicitly that Alexander had to be led back to Rome by an armed force provided by Frederick.

Having listed all the many instances in which Boso stuck to the truth although it did not really suit his preconceived dramatic purpose, we next turn to all those cases where Boso told a half truth. After the fall of Milan in 1162, of which Boso incidentally makes very little, Frederick decided to seek an end to the schism. Boso reports truthfully the importance which Frederick attached to this task: but adds that Frederick did so because he was 'confused and terrified by the accusations of his conscience'. It is true that this picture of Frederick fits in with Boso's drama. But the explanation of Frederick's desire to end the schism at this particular point given by Boso is not borne out by the evidence. The real truth is that Frederick was told by his diplomats he could not hope to pacify

[65] P. Munz, 'Frederick Barbarossa and Henry the Lion in 1176', *Historical Studies*, XII, 1965   [66] See note 53 above.
[67] Romuald of Salerno, *Annales*, MGH, *SS*, 19, p. 447, lines 9ff.

C

Lombardy as long as Alexander, seeking to oppose Frederick's Pope Victor, kept fomenting resistance in Lombardy. Frederick's real reason for wishing to end the schism was not his bad conscience but the politic consideration that his military victory in Lombardy was likely to remain hollow as long as Alexander kept acting like a magnet for all disaffection and rebellion.[68] Boso, although he is quite truthful in relating the extortions and oppression caused by Frederick's vicars and commissioners in Lombardy in the early sixties,[69] is not telling the whole truth because he omits to mention that in the late fifties a great many cities had been ready to go along with Frederick's proposal to establish imperial government and administration in Milan.[70] The truth is that the oppressions which Boso relates were an unfortunate consequence of the continued opposition of Lombardy, led and inspired by Alexander and his legates. Boso's drama, however, forces him to make out that oppression in Lombardy was the key-note of Frederick's Lombard policy throughout. Even so, in one place, Boso states emphatically that at first Frederick had hoped to be 'loved' by the Lombards and states that the imperial rule in Lombardy began to be a 'burden' only *after* the destruction of Milan in 1162. He, therefore, only partially seeks to hide the fact that Frederick's intentions in Lombardy had originally been good and had nothing to do with the schism and that things had started to go wrong only after 1162.

Boso is also guilty of a half-truth in his report of the election of Victor's successor in Lucca in 1164. There is no reason to doubt his version of the actual election. But his failure to mention Rainald von Dassel's role distorts the matter completely. The rushed election was engineered by Rainald[71] and Frederick actually disapproved[72]

---

[68] FB, p. 226f.

[69] For details see F. Güterbock, 'Markward von Grumbach', *Mitteilungen des Instituts f. oesterreichische Geschichtsforschung*, 48, 1934, p. 39 and the same author's 'Alla vigilia della Lega Lombarda', *Archivio storico italiano*, 95, 1937. Cp. also *Annales Mediolanenses*, MGH, *Scriptores*, 18, p. 376 and the material collected by J. Ficker, *Forschungen zur Reichs— und Rechtsgeschichte Italiens*, 1961 reprint, II, pp. 107ff.

[70] FB, p. 163f.

[71] Rainald's role comes out clearly in *Annales Pisani ad 1165*, MGH, *Scriptores*, 19, p. 250. Cp. J. Ficker, *Rainald von Dassel*, Köln, 1850, p. 55.

[72] For Frederick's disapproval of Rainald's impetuous action see *Rad. De Diceto Ymaginibus Historiarum*, MGH, *Scriptores*, 27, p. 263 and W. v. Giescebrecht, *Geschichte der deutschen Kaiserzeit*, 2nd ed., Braunschweig, 1877-., Vol. V. p. 397.

because he saw in Victor's death a chance for ending the schism. But having cast Frederick in the role of the villain Boso could not afford to mention Frederick's instructions for caution which, accidentally, reached Rainald too late. Similarly, he truthfully reports the disastrous Roman defeat at Tusculum which immediately preceded Frederick's conquest of Rome. But again he does not mention Rainald who personally was the victor and who lost no time in telling the whole world of his military prowess.[73] Boso is guilty of another half-truth in his account of Frederick's conquest of Rome in 1167. He does not conceal Frederick's military triumph and, as we have seen, makes rightly the most of the atrocities that were committed. But he does fail to report that, after all, Frederick came to terms with the Romans, led his own Pope, Paschal III, into the city and had himself crowned Emperor a second time. This victory for Frederick is passed over in silence because it would have looked too much as if God, after all, was, at least for one brief moment, on the side of the schismatics. To report this fact would have marred the starkness of the dramatic conflict between villain and hero. Boso, incidentally, is equally silent about another, perhaps somewhat empty triumph for Frederick which had taken place the year before in Aix-la-Chapelle, the canonization of Charlemagne. The next half-truth concerns the peace mission led by Eberhard of Bamberg. Boso is quite informative about the mission and even admits its chances of success because Eberhard of Bamberg was such a 'good catholic'. But, guided by his conception that the story was a fight between a villain and a hero, Boso cannot give credit to Frederick for honest intentions in regard to this mission. Having admitted Eberhard's catholicism, he ought to have given Frederick the benefit of doubt, to say the least, for having chosen a man like Eberhard. Eberhard himself, and of this there can be no doubt, was convinced of Frederick's sincerity. For otherwise he would not have allowed himself to be sent. He had been one of Frederick's close advisers at the beginning of the reign. But in the late fifties and especially at the beginning of the schism, he had voluntarily withdrawn from Frederick's counsels because he could not reconcile the new policy with his conscience. Eberhard's integrity was above

---

[73] For the good press which Rainald gives himself after the battle of Tusculum see P. Munz, 'Frederick Barbarossa and the "Holy Empire"', *Journal of Religious History*, Vol. III, 1964, p. 35, note 40.

suspicion[74] and in this case, Boso ought to have admitted that it reflected on Frederick. When we come to the end of the story, Boso is guilty of another half-truth. He tells us that after the battle of Legnano (1176) Cremona suddenly defected from the League 'without serious cause'. Boso must have known quite well what the serious cause was. Cremona defected because Frederick's military strength was unimpaired and quite formidable and the good citizens of Cremona, having tarried for some time, decided not to take risks. Finally, in his account of the Venice peace negotiations, Boso again makes no mention of Frederick's military strength in Romagna and in the territory encompassed by the Matildan lands.[75] Soon after, however, he admits that it was agreed at Venice that Frederick should remain in possession of the Matildan lands and provide the badly needed military escort for Alexander's return to Rome.[76] Boso, in other words, tells the story quite correctly. Frederick was in militay occupation of these lands and there was nothing Alexander could do about it. And although Boso admits Alexander's need for military escort and thus reveals Alexander's dependence on Frederick's protection, he conceals the fact of actual military possession so that he can say that Alexander agreed to Frederick's retention of the Matildan lands out of the goodness of his heart.

Finally, we come to the complete falsehoods. Some were probably due to ignorance or even carelessness; for no historian is completely infallible. But it has to be admitted that a great many of these falsehoods are so manifestly suitable to Boso's dramatic plot, that it is difficult to attribute them to accident. First and foremost, Boso is quite wrong in stating that the Council of Pavia in 1160 which decided in favour of Victor was packed and that the decision was a foregone conclusion and part of Frederick's plot to cause a schism. The Acts of the Council and a great many other observers tell a very different story. Frederick summoned bishops from all over Christendom. Alexander refused to attend because, understandably, he did not trust Frederick. As a result his case was badly put. At any rate, Victor did have some case because he could make out that he had been elected by popular acclamation. And with Alexander refusing to counter Victor's claim in person, Frederick chose the

[74] P. Munz, 'Why did Rahewin stop writing the Gesta Frederici?' *English Historical Review*, LXXXIV, 1969, p. 772.

[75] FB, p. 328 for literature and sources.

[76] FB, p. 363 for literature and sources.

way of least resistance and confirmed Victor.[77] Boso also, in spite of his later accounts, gives initially a false description of the foundation of Alcssandria. In the first instance, he declares in very high-sounding terms that the city was founded as a stronghold against Frederick. We know, partly from his own later admissions, that this was not true.[78] It was not only that the city of Alessandria was not as properly fortified as it would have been had it been founded as a symbol of defiance. Boso states that Frederick decided to destroy Alessandria in 1174, not in order to teach the Lombards a lesson but because the Markgrave of Monferrato and Pavia, at whose expense the city had grown, had asked him to. Moreover, Boso tells that the Lombards came to Alessandria's assistance only after four months— hardly a credible story if Alessandria was a symbol of resistance. He also tells us that Pope Alexander made Alessandria a bishopric only after the city's successful resistance to Frederick. If Alessandria had been founded as a symbol and named after him, it is very improbable that Alexander would have tarried so long.

Boso is also completely untrustworthy in his account of Alexander's reaction to the news of the murder of Thomas Becket. Alexander's relations with Thomas Becket do not figure in the story at all. Like so many other things that happened to Alexander, they had no direct bearing on the schism. Moreover, Boso had a special reason for playing down the whole unfortunate Becket affair. Alexander, throughout the quarrel between Henry II and Becket, had been very politic

---

[77] MGH, *Legum Sectio IV*, I, Nos. 188–190. It is only fair to add that Boso and Alexander were not alone in their contempt for Pavia. Cp. e.g. William of Newburgh, *Hist. Ang.*, ii, 9; John of Salisbury, W. J. Millor, H. E. Butler, and C. N. L. Brooke eds., *The Letters of John of Salisbury*, London, 1955, Vol. I, No. 124. John's statement, however, lets the cat out of the bag and is worth quoting. He says that 'the absent were condemned without examination of their cause' (p. 206). This is a patent untruth and contradicted by the report in MGH, *loc. cit.*, No. 190, c.1–2, where it is clearly stated that Alexander's case was not only heard and examined but also that Alexander had the vote of the majority of cardinals, albeit not of the 'saner part'. John of Salisbury, uneasily conscious of this, continues, therefore thus: '. . . or rather I should say, in a cause which should not have been examined either in that place or in that fashion or by such judges . . .'. It was one thing to state that Alexander's case was not heard; and quite another to argue that it was heard but ought not to have been heard by certain people. John meant the end of his sentence to be a mere qualification of the beginning. But in fact it is a contradiction of the beginning.

[78] See note 63 above.

33

and circumspect. He could not afford to alienate Henry as well as Frederick and he had therefore not taken a heroic stand in favour of Becket. In order to present Alexander consistently as a hero, Boso would have had to twist the facts too much. He, therefore, preferred to gloss the matter over and confine himself to merely distorting the end of the story. In the middle sixties, King Henry II of England had briefly flirted with Frederick, for he felt that his problems with Thomas Becket were very similar to Frederick's problems with Alexander. And at one crucial moment, at the Court of Würzburg (1165) when Frederick and many of his princes and bishops were on the verge of giving in to Alexander, it was the sudden arrival of the news that Henry of England might join the schismatics officially which swung opinion once more against Alexander and led to the notorious and impolitic oath against him. Thus the news of Thomas Becket's murder, which reached Alexander in Tusculum on the Thursday before Easter 1172, *was* part of Boso's story. But his version of Alexander's reaction is untruthful. Boso makes out that Henry II was falling over himself with remorse and fear and begged Alexander to forgive him. Boso also tells that Henry dropped everything he was then doing in order to meet the papal envoys and prostrate himself. Alexander, true shepherd that he was, accepted Henry's protestations of personal innocence and his promises to atone for any indirect responsibility he may have had. The truth is very different. 'Alexander was not prepared to rescue Henry's reputation'. Negotiations were slow and embassies went to and fro. It is true that according to some, Henry made a great display of sorrow. But it is also true that he did not drop everything else to wait upon the Pope's word but that, on the contrary, when he 'received bad news from Ireland [he] took the opportunity thus offered of disappearing from an awkward situation . . . and remained at a distance till he was recalled early in 1172 by the threatened revolt of his sons'. It was then and then only that the 'impending catastrophe drove him to seek peace with the Church'.[79] Nothing of all this in Boso. Boso had one villain and one villain only. All the other Kings of Christendom, including the hard-headed Henry of England, were faithful and obedient and penitent. The extent of Boso's misrepresentation of Henry II is very remarkable. Henry's personal display of sorrow was true enough, whatever his

[79] D. Knowles, *Thomas Becket*, London, 1970, pp. 150ff.

precise motives for the display.[80] But Boso is quite wrong in saying that Henry had given his envoy authority to make a number of sworn promises to Alexander. The envoys, when they discovered the extent of Alexander's anger about the murder, took it upon themselves to make promises in order to avoid a complete diplomatic catastrophe.[81] This puts a completely different light on Henry from the one in which Boso wished him to appear. It is also wrong of Boso to say that on his return from Ireland, Henry rushed to meet the papal envoys 'humbly and with reverence', ready to abide by their command.[82]

Next we come to Frederick's rapprochement with the Lombards. Boso tells in graphic detail how Frederick suffered a severe military set-back at the hands of Alessandria and decided as a result of this defeat to make peace. The truth is that Frederick had very solid extraneous reasons for making peace and had been drawn, possibly even against his better judgement, into the siege of Alessandria. He had laid siege to the city to please two of his allies who resented the growth of that city, Pavia and the Markgrave of Monferrato, at whose expense the city had grown. Boso, for that matter, makes no bones about the role of Pavia and the Markgrave. But his dramatic conception obliged him to show that, eventually, God caused Frederick to be beaten. He could not allow any other reason for a change of policy. Similarly, Boso's account of the battle of Legnano is quite wrong in outline, even though many details, such as the story that the Germans lost heart when Frederick was thrown off his horse, appear quite correct. The battle was not a military defeat. It is true that the Lombards at first thought so. But it is equally true and borne out by subsequent events, that although the Germans fled,

[80] It is worth noting that according to Boso, Henry said that he was as 'grief-stricken and sorrowful as if I had learnt that my own son had been slain'. According to the witness in Robertson and Sheppard, *Materials for the History of Thomas Becket*, London, 1885, Vol. VII, No. 771, p. 514, Henry said that he 'had not been so grieved by the death of his father and mother'.

[81] The steps taken by Henry's envoys are reported in Robertson and Sheppard, *op. cit.*, Vol. VII, No. 750, p. 474 and No. 751, p. 477. J. Haller and D. Knowles differ somewhat in their emphasis. Haller, *Das Papsttum*, Stuttgart, 1952, III, p. 220 writes that Henry's envoys 'exceeded their instructions and claimed to have been ordered...'. D. Knowles, *Thomas Becket*, London, 1970, p. 151, using exactly the same source, says nothing more than that the envoys engaged 'themselves on behalf of the King to obey...'.

[82] 'Henry was truculent and would not swear to do all that the Pope might command him'. D. Knowles, *Thomas Becket*, London, 1970, p. 152.

they were not wiped out. Frederick's military position after the battle remained very strong and if he decided on a renewal of peace negotiations, it was not because he had been vanquished on the battlefield.[83]

The last example which shows that Boso allowed himself to be carried away from the truth by the overriding considerations of his plot is provided by his story that 'at the Pope's peaceful and so long looked-for return there was very great rejoicing in the city of Rome'. It is true that the drama demanded to be concluded on some such note. From a literary point of view, this is a perfect counter-point to the opening scenes in which Alexander, though the rightful and canonically elected Pope, had to steal away from the city under cover of darkness and in fear for his life. But the truth is that Alexander was escorted back to Rome by Christian, the Archbishop of Mainz, Frederick's chief military commander; and that he could maintain himself in Rome only because and so long as Christian and his armed men kept terrorizing the countryside.[84] Only before the very end, for one brief moment, Boso the historian prevails once more over Boso the dramatist and we are told that Alexander himself had great doubts about the Romans and 'not unnaturally hesitated to believe in their fine promises'.

It is futile as well as impossible to turn the question of Boso's trustworthiness and of his value as a historian into a statistical problem and weigh the truths, the half-truths and the falsehoods in a fine balance. All things considered, then, Boso's history of the schism is a fine piece of historical writing and stands head and shoulders above the other contributions of the *Liber Pontificalis*. But the stature of the work is due to its dramatic quality—a quality which lends a methodical and systematic distortion to the whole account. At the same time, like so many other historical works that betray their literary structure, it is a unique source of information. Much of it has been corroborated by other sources and other parts, as most readers will easily detect, have gone whole into all recognized and established historical accounts of the period. It is by no means Boso's least merit that his very dramatization of the story should today be able to help us to spot the reasons for the resulting distortions. The reasons for this particular perspective, because so very contemporary, throw an important and invaluable light on both Boso and his friend

[83] FB, pp. 310ff.   [84] FB, pp. 363ff.

Alexander. We are, indeed, obliged to believe that Alexander himself thought of his long resistance in this dramatic fashion and most probably derived the emotional drive which enabled him to weather the storm from this way of looking at himself and his task. Had he been less flamboyant, he would have caved in. Sobriety is a great virtue; but is more likely to lead to despair and scepticism than to almost superhuman tenaciousness and perseverance. The distortion of vision never led to blind fanaticism. But the dramatic perspective in which Alexander and his closest supporters seem to have seen themselves and interpreted their misfortunes, provided just sufficient stamina for eighteen years of dogged resistance, more often than not accompanied by gruesome personal physical deprivation. Without this self-dramatization, one of the most powerfully influential and institutionally creative Popes of the middle ages, might not have been able to survive the trying circumstances of his pontificate.

If we can learn some of the reasons for Alexander's tenaciousness and for his success from Boso's way of seeing him, we can also learn something very important about Alexander from the things Boso does not say. First of all, it is remarkable that Boso's manner of writing history shows nothing of the influence of John of Salisbury whose *Historia Pontificalis* covers part of the period immediately preceding the period about which Boso writes. The lack of John of Salisbury's influence is all the more remarkable as John was as devoted and outspoken a partisan of Alexander as Boso himself. John was a consummate stylist with a vivid interest in human affairs. Although he shows the ecclesiastical historian's conventional interest in the privileges of the archbishopric of Canterbury, he devotes most of his attention to an ironical description of St. Bernard's efforts to condemn the teachings of Gilbert de la Porrée and, later, offers us a genuinely perceptive portrait of that famous ecclesiastic, Henry, the Bishop of Winchester. There is an air of detachment and subtle understanding of human foibles in John of Salisbury's history. By comparison, Boso's drama of the clash between good and evil is a monolithic stereotype. Although John of Salisbury, at the time of the Council of Pavia proved one of Alexander's staunchest defenders, the gulf that separates Boso's story from John's way of writing history would seem to indicate that Boso and Alexander carried on their struggle against Frederick Barbarossa in a spirit far removed from the humanism of John of Salisbury. Furthermore, writing his story about Alexander the hero and Frederick the villain in the way

37

he did, Boso also took his conscious distance from another way of looking on history which was widely current in the twelfth century and the greatest monument of which was Otto of Freising's *Chronicle of the Two Cities*. In this Chronicle, Otto described the course of history from the great days of the Christianized Roman Empire to the Investiture struggle at the end of the eleventh century as the history of a *civitas permixta,* of a mixed community. In this community, church and empire had been at one and well 'mixed'. From the end of the eleventh century onwards, however, the separation of the one from the other had begun and as good people (Cistercian monks and crusaders, in the main) were drawing away from evil people, the city of God and the city of the devil were gradually being separated. As the evil people were being left to their own devices, the reign of the Antichrist was being prepared and the moment in which history would end, was drawing near. In this philosophy of history we can detect clear anticipations of Joachimism as well as the strong influence of the great symbolist theologians of the twelfth century, Honorius Augustodunensis and Anselm of Havelberg.[85] Eventually, under the impact of Frederick Barbarossa, Otto of Freising was to change his mind during the fifties of the twelfth century and produce his own book on Frederick, written in a completely different spirit.[86] But for our present purposes it is remarkable that Boso too, when he wrote his history of Alexander III, took no cognizance of the conventional symbolist interpretation of history. There is nothing about the Antichrist in his work and nothing about the approaching end of history.[87] There are no echoes of St. Augustine's two cities. The current philosophy of history did not suit Boso any more than it suited Alexander's rational temper. They were freely given to emotional self-dramatization; but would not

[85] There is a vast literature on these philosophers or theologians of history, but nothing as clear and penetrating as M.–D. Chenu, *Nature, Man and Society in the Twelfth Century*, Chicago and London, 1968, Ch. 5.

[86] See FB, pp. 130ff.

[87] Alexander himself was, naturally, not unaware of the great vogue of Antichrist speculation. If we take Boso's work as an indication of his reasoned assessment of his struggle and his role in history, he did not take this vogue too seriously. But this is not to say that he did not avail himself of it for propaganda purposes when it suited him. In his manifesto of early October 1159, issued immediately after the double election and widely distributed (Jaffé-Löwenfeld, *Regesta Pontificum Romanorum*, Leipzig, 1885–8, II, Nos. 10586–92), he proclaimed that 'Octavian represented the age of the Antichrist'.

indulge in metaphysical speculation or attempts to see themselves in terms of the great cosmic struggle between the two cities and make use of symbolism in order to interpret the role they were playing in that struggle. The long distance which separates Boso from the other historical thinkers of the twelfth century, from Otto of Freising's earlier work and from Honorius Augustodunensis as well as from Anselm of Havelberg and, eventually, from Joachim of Fiore (c. 1135 to 1202) is important and telling evidence for the world in which Pope Alexander lived and thought and carried on his long struggle against Frederick.

Boso's Life of
Alexander III

Alexander III is a Tuscan, a native of Siena, the son of Rainucci. His original name was Roland, and as Cardinal Priest of St. Mark, he was Chancellor of the Apostolic See. His pontificate has lasted eighteen years. Because of his great fame in the Church of Pisa, where all had held him dear and in high renown, he was summoned by Pope Eugene of blessed memory to this Church at Rome. When the Holy Father under divine impulse considered him ready, he raised him first to the rank of Cardinal Deacon, of the title of SS. Comas and Damian, and then made him Cardinal Priest, of St. Mark, and finally, since Roland continued to go from one great achievement to another, the pope appointed him to the office of Chancellor of the Holy See. Roland is a man of great eloquence, well enough learned in the writings of both human and divine authors, and skilled by careful practice in the understanding of them; moreover he is a man of the Schools, ready in the ways of polite speaking, at once thoughtful, kind, patient, merciful, gentle, sober, chaste, assiduous in the bestowing of alms, and ever intent on performing all the other good works that please God. As a result 'the Lord made him increase among his people and gave him a great priesthood'.

After the burial of Pope Hadrian of happy memory, the Bishops and Cardinals who were to elect his successor in the pastorate assembled on 4 September in St. Peter's, and for three days deliberated, in the customary way, about their choice. At length all present, with the exception of the Cardinal Priests Octavian of St. Cecilia, John of St. Martin, and Guy of St. Callixtus, were inspired by God to give a unanimous decision for the person of the Chancellor, Roland. Invoking the favour of the Holy Spirit, and with the assent of the clergy and people, they nominated Roland and chose him to be Pope of the Roman See, Alexander III. (But two of those whom I have just named, John and Guy, eager for the election of Octavian, made so bold as to give their nomination to him.) With divine assent the Cardinal Bishop of Ostia, together with those of Albano, Porto, and Sabina, and the other Cardinals, Priests and

43

Deacons, according to the ancient ritual of the Church made the Prior of the Deacons place the Papal mantle on him who was their choice. He drew back, making his excuses. He appeared unwilling and wholly reluctant. But Octavian, who had long aspired to the Chair of the Apostle, on seeing himself disappointed in his hope, was moved to such a peak of madness and rashness that he snatched the mantle like a robber, tore it with his own hands from Alexander's shoulders, and attempted among cries and confusion to carry it off. But one of the Senators who was in attendance, seeing so terrible a crime, was moved to anger, and throwing himself bodily on the ranting man, siezed the mantle from his hands. Octavian was stung to the heart by his disappointment. He glanced around immediately for his Chaplain, who had come both aware of and ready for this moment, and bellowing out like a lunatic beckoned to him to bring quickly the mantle which he, Octavian, had kept by. This he brought without delay, and since none of the Cardinals present was of his cause, Octavian, taking off his cap and bowing his head, impudently, alas! with the aid of his Chaplain and another cleric, put on the mantle. But it happened by the judgement of God that that part of the mantle which should have fallen over the front of his body covered his back—which all saw and laughed at—and the more he tried to correct the cause of so much mockery, the more he, beside himself at not being able to find the cowl, got the hem of the garment twisted around his neck. It was perfectly clear from this that, just as his mind was twisted and his intentions devious, he wore his mantle awry in testimony of his own condemnation. And now the doors of the Church, which had been defended by the Senators, were closed behind Octavian as he went forth blinded by his ambition. But he had hired bands of armed men and now they ran in a great hubbub and with drawn swords to the aid of the schismatic. Since there was no help forthcoming to him from the Bishops and Cardinals, Octavian surrounded himself on all sides with mobs of armed men.

When his brethren saw a crime so detestable, and one unheard of for many centuries, they were afraid that they too would be forced to adore the idol that had been set up. Accordingly they withdrew with the man of their choice within the walls of the church. There the antipope shut them up for nine days. There was no way for them to escape. Day and night, with the connivance of certain Senators whom Octavian had suborned by gifts of money, Octavian kept them closely confined with an armed band. But while this was going on, the people of Rome kept up such a constant cry against so much wickedness and such a muttering against these Senators that the Pope-elect and his brother Bishops broke out of their sanctuary, but only to be carried off like animals to a more confined and closely guarded place in Trastevere by those Senators in return for further sums of money. But when they had languished there for nearly three days, the whole city was thrown into a tumult over such a criminal act and so clear a betrayal. Children cried out against the usurper in the Church: 'Accursed son of an accursed father,* you cloak-room thief, you shan't be Pope, you shan't be Pope', and 'We choose Alexander, the choice of God'. Women too reviled Octavian as a heretic, shouted the same remarks after him and lampooned him in song. A certain Britto went up to him and boldy recited the following verses:

> Octavian, you madman, you're your country's bane;
> Why do you dare to tear Christ's tunic?
> Soon dust you'll be, today alive, tomorrow dead.

Great distress came over the clergy and sorrow over the judges. Old men felt grief, the ordinary folk amazement. And so it happened that the Roman people were unable any longer to tolerate the pressing burden of so great an evil. They came with Otto Frangipani and other Roman nobles to the brethren's place of detention, and compelled the Senators to open speedily the doors of their fortress and let Pope Alexander and his brethren depart freely and without hindrance. And so through the intercession of the holy Apostles Peter and Paul they were delivered from the violence of the persecutor and set free.

Passing in honour through the city itself, with songs of praise and the bells pealing everywhere at their welcome delivery, and with both a great company of the Roman soldiery and a concourse of infantry, they came safely on the eve of St. Matthew's day by divine Providence to Ninfa. And there, on that very Sunday, with all his brethren assembled—to wit, Gregory, Cardinal Bishop of St. Sabina, Theobald of Ostia, Bernard of Porto, Walter of Albano, John of Segnia, and Bernard of Terracina, and the Cardinal Priests and Deacons—with the abbots, priors, judges, advocates, notaries, the

---

*A pun on Octavian's family name Maledictus.

precentor with the *schola cantorum*, the nobles, and a very great part of the people of Rome, the lord Alexander received the consecration of a Supreme Pontiff whose election has been ratified by the Holy Spirit, and was crowned according to the rites of the Church with the symbol of Papal authority by the Cardinal Bishop of Ostia, to whom alone the duty of the consecration of a Supreme Pontiff belongs.

Thereupon Octavian, with the intention of confirming his rash and presumptuous action, both while he was at St. Peter's and after his secret departure from the Leonine City, summoned to himself many Bishops. Some of these he sought to attract to his cause by threatening them with the Emperor, others by the violent acts of laymen, and others again by bribery and blandishments. But all this effort was to no purpose, since the Lord opposed him. But the false brethren I. of Morrone and Guy of Crema, having been reminded while wreathed in the darkness of their blindness that, as it is written, 'the sinner, when he shall come to the depth of his sins, shall be downcast', did not return to their senses from their damnable presumption, but with a stubborn perfidy worshipped him whom they had raised up as an idol for themselves, and left, alas! the unity of the Church and bent their ways to follow in his footprints. But Octavian, foreshadowing the days of Antichrist, was so raised up above himself as to sit, like a Papal wraith in God's Temple, displaying himself as if he were truly Pope. Many looked upon the abomination standing in the holy place not without tears in their eyes, striking their breasts and saying: 'Now has come to pass what Pope Anastasius is said to have told Octavian as one who foreshadows Antichrist to his face: "Son of an accursed and excommunicate father, you will never have that papal mantle that you so desire and so brazenly seek except to your confusion and the destruction of many"'.

But when he had wearied himself throughout the space of four weeks in calling Bishops to his side, not only by his own efforts but by those of the military power, and those of his own kith and kin, and when all still shrank from taking a stand with him, a certain fellow, the Bishop of Melfi so-called, a fugitive and outlaw who lurked in the March of Ancona, with the Bishop of Ferentino—an opponent of Pope Hadrian—and the Bishop of Tusculum, Imar, a former supporter of Alexander but now estranged from him: these three then, now excommunicate after second and third warnings, consecrated Octavian with brazen presumption. As later became obvious, Octavian would have had no part in initiating so pernicious an attack on the Church of God, had he not found the favour and support of the Emperor Frederick for his plan of having or at least seizing the Papacy. It was believed and not without evidence, that Octavian had bound himself to Frederick by an oath of fealty to be able to mount the papal throne by whatever means he could.

While these events were occurring, Alexander went down to Terracina with his brother Bishops. He was eager to learn what the Count Palatine Otto and Guy, Count of Biandrate would do about these matters in the Church. These were the men whom the Emperor had sent on a mission to Pope Hadrian of blessed memory. But though they were fully aware of what had happened, and could not have any doubts that Alexander's election was canonical, they were afraid to give offence to their lord. They knew that the Emperor and Octavian were on terms of the greatest friendship. They had had knowledge of the way his mind was moving against the Roman Church. So they made great display to Octavian of their favour and support while at the same time entering deceitfully into consultations with Alexander.

During the course of these events, the Pontiff took counsel with his brother Bishops, and in humility directed Apostolic letters to the Emperor, who was at that time laying siege to Crema, a town of Lombardy. In all patience and meekness, he besought him to return to his love for the Church with the words of the blessed Apostle Paul: 'Be not overcome by evil, but overcome evil with good'. The Emperor full of pride and disdain, not only would not accept the letter, but also like a madman would have hanged the Papal envoys in violation of their immunity, had not Duke Welf and the Duke of Saxony prevented him. Although, yielding to the advice and persuasion of his Princes, Frederick allowed the envoys to come before him and had, at long last, the letters read to him, he did not deign to reply to the Pontiff. He was of the opinion that it was possible to take away from the Church the privilege of liberty granted it by our Lord Himself and that he could set a Pope on the throne of the Apostle Peter just as he saw fit. And so the Emperor sent two of his supporters, the Bishops of Verden and Prague to those Bishops who had accompanied Pope Alexander to Anagni. His letter to them was not a letter of the Church's protector and defender, but a letter of its superior judge and master with power over them. Their journey to Anagni was swiftly made and exhibited all the signs of pride for when they entered the palace and stood before the Pope, who was there with all his brethren, and many others both clerks and layfolk, they made him no obeisance. They read out the messages their lord had charged them with, and handed over a letter sealed with gold. The tenor of its contents was that the Emperor, hearing of the dissension which swirled about the Church of Rome, had called on churchmen from five kingdoms and on behalf of the universal Church had instructed them to assemble before him at Pavia on the octave of the Epiphany to give hearing and heed to what would be there decided.

At this the brethren were troubled, and on account of the grave evils that pressed in upon them from every side, they felt very fearful and anxious. For some the greatest fear was the persecution at the hands of so powerful a prince that loomed over them, for others, the violations and utter destruction of the Church's liberty. There was fear too of creating a precedent that would be the ruin of other Churches.

Besides, the fact that the Emperor, in his letter, spoke of Octavian as the Pontiff of Rome and of Alexander as the Pope of the Chancelleries did little to dispel the sadness that afflicted the hearts of his brethren. On these matters therefore they held a long discussion with much dispute and argument. At length, inspired by God from whom all good things proceed, all were so strengthened in their belief in Catholic unity and in their obedience to their Pontiff, that one by one they freely offered, in maintenance of the liberty of the Church, to undergo the perils of death itself, should that be required of them. And now since Verden and Prague were pressing him for an answer, Pope Alexander dictated this letter before a great number of clerks and layfolk:

We acknowledge that the Emperor, by the duty imposed upon him by his office, is the protector and particular guardian of the holy Roman Church. For this reason we strive to give his person honour above that accorded to every other prince of the world, even when it is not strictly his due, and to defer to him in every matter which gives no offence to the honour of the King of kings. But when anything occurs which cannot but slight the highest King, it seems that the emperor of the earth must be honoured in such a way, that He should be feared above all, and His honour maintained Who is King of kings and Lord of lords, Who has dominion over the whole earth and Who can destroy both body and soul in Hell. We are surprised therefore that while we display a sincere and filial respect for the Emperor we receive no sincere affection from him, and that while we wish to show his excellence greater honour, we see that due honour is denied by him to us, the most lowly successor of blessed Peter, and to the holy Roman Church. For in the letter which you have brought our brethren and us from him, there was this expression among others: 'He, because he had heard of the dissension which had overwhelmed the Church of Rome, had summoned churchmen from five kingdoms, and instructed them on behalf of the Universal Church to appear before him at Pavia on the octave of the Epiphany, to hear and pay heed to the decisions of that Council'. In this matter he seems to have abandoned the custom of his predecessors, and to have overstepped the bounds of his office, since he has summoned a Council without the Bishop of Rome having knowledge of it and like one having power over us, has bidden us to appear before him. But is it not correct that it was to Blessed Peter, and afterwards from him to the holy Roman Church of which he is by the power of God the teacher and founder, that this privilege was in lawful fashion handed down from the Lord Jesus Christ and the holy Fathers? And is it not correct that both in prosperity and adversity it has been maintained to this day, even to the point of bloodshed if necessary, that when the occasion demanded, Peter's authority would examine and finalize matters pertaining to every Church, but that its own should be subject to the judgements of none? For this reason, because we now see an insult contrary to the privilege of the Church made by him who ought to be defending it against the attacks of others, and because a letter has been written to his Mother as if she were one of his subjects, we neither are able to nor ought to tolerate this without the greatest surprise. We are not allowed by either canonical tradition or the revered authority of the holy Fathers to attend this Council or to accept decision in this matter. In the lesser Churches the attorneys and the secular prince do not usurp for themselves and their own courts the summoning of witnesses, legal arguments, and decisions in cases of this sort, but await the cognizance and decision of their Metropolitans or the Apostolic See. Accordingly it would seem the more worthy of God's concern and the more worthy of greater censure by the Universal Church the more it redounded to its peril, if we allowed that disease to take hold in our days in the Church through our ignorance and a weakness of spirit in its very head (which God forbid), and allowed the Church, ransomed by the Precious Blood of Christ, to be reduced to slavery in our days. It is for that Church for whom our predecessors in defence of its freedom shed their own blood that we ourselves ought, in imitation of them, undergo the most dreadful dangers, should the exigencies of the moment require it.

When this reply had been given, the Bishops who had been sent on the embassy were wroth, and returning in anger, came before Octavian at Segni. So too did Otto, the Count Palatine, and those Germans whom the Emperor had sent as envoys in his company to the territories of the City. Then the heart of the heresiarch himself was not a little elated, and, beside himself in his emotion like the blind fool he was, he grew greatly puffed up by pride, not knowing that, according to the words of the blessed martyr Cyprian, schismatics are in the beginning all ardour, but ever have no development, nor can they profit by their unlawful gains, but straightway fail in their wicked and jealous rivalry. It is of ambitious men such as these that the prophet speaks when he says: 'Truly because of their deceits thou hast dealt harshly with them; thou hast cast them down while they were being raised on high. How were they made desolate? On a sudden they failed and perished on account of their iniquities like the dream of one rising from sleep.' Such ones moreover the Apostle John curses and smites with these words: 'They went out from us, but they were not of us, for had they been of us, they would have remained with us.' For this reason heresies frequently have arisen and will continue to arise as long as perverse minds are not at peace and faithlessness which disrupts does not hold fast to unity. But God permits these things to happen and tolerates them, while all the time preserving the exercise of His own freedom, so that, when He examines our hearts and minds with the judgement of His truth, the pure faith of the just may shine through with a clear light. The Holy Spirit also forewarns us through the words of the Apostle, and says: 'There must be heresies and schisms, that they who are reckoned worthy may be made manifest among you.' So are the faithful tried, and the faithless discovered. But let us return to our subject.

The Emperor Frederick, vainly hoping to be able to bring to fruition the evil conceit which he had long had of subjecting the Church of Christ to his own power, summoned the heretic to attend him in Lombardy, and gathering together as many Bishops and other clerks as he could from the lands under his dominion, went to Pavia, with the intention of holding there with Octavian a General Council. At that town he revealed his sacrilegious intention and abominable plan with sly cunning. He asserted that Pope Alexander and his brother Bishops and associates were the enemies of the Empire and of his person and had plotted with those who hated and opposed him, but that Octavian had ever been faithful and in all matters devoted to himself and his rule. It seemed to the Emperor that for this reason Octavian's election, though made by a smaller number of Catholic Bishops, should secure the grace and favour of the Empire rather than the bold deed of many conspirators. Therefore to secure the obedience and submission to Octavian of those who had assembled, on some he showered favours and promises, but on others, who were unwilling, threats and terrors. And so, to the ruin of his own soul and the destruction of many others, in his attempt to tear the seamless robe of Christ, that is the unity of the Catholic Faith, the Emperor was the first to bow low before the feet of Octavian himself and forced as many others as he could to do the same.

When this had been done he published an edict throughout the whole of his dominions: prelates were to make their obeisance at the foot of the idol which he had had raised up and whoever was not of a mind to do so, was to go forth from his dominions, never to return. Throughout the whole of Italy the word of this man, hard and bitter, was heard. Every man of ardent spirit chose rather to endure exile and persecution for God's sake and the maintenance of his faith whole and entire, than to become in peace the adherent of schismatics with their honours, and have in plenty the riches of this world. In the Church of God there was great distress. Catholics fled and left their Churches, their families and their homeland deserted and Octavian's accomplices took over their places with violence.

But when the blessed Pope Alexander in spite of gentle and frequent pleas could by no means win back the Emperor from his faithlessness, on Maundy Thursday at Anagni he, with the Bishops and Cardinals, solemnly placed on Frederick the ban of excommunication as the chief persecutor of the Church of God. All who were bound to Frederick by oath of fealty, in accordance with the ancient custom of his predecessors, were absolved from their oaths. He also renewed the sentence of excommunication already passed on Octavian and his associates. Since, moreover, the very schismatics, lacking faith in either justice or truth, had ensnared the prelates of the churches and the princes of the world with cunning contrivances of lies and had tried to make them side with their error, it seemed a useful counsel to the Pope that he should send some of his brethren as legates *a latere* to the various regions of the world. Only by their

zeal and labours would enlightenment come about the facts of the
election to the Apostolic See, and the whole body of faithful, once
the truth was known, be made united and firm in their trust in
Catholic unity. To France were sent therefore Henry, Cardinal
Priest of St. Nereus, William, Cardinal Priest of St. Peter-ad-
Vincula, and Master Odo, Cardinal Deacon of St. Nicholas in
Carcere; to the Latin Patriarchate of the East, John, Cardinal of SS.
John and Paul; to Hungary, Julius, Bishop of Praeneste and Peter,
Cardinal Deacon of St. Eustachius; and to the Emperor at Con-
stantinople, the Bishop of Tivoli and Ardicio, Cardinal Deacon of
St. Theodore.

When the truth of the election had been widely published abroad
and was known without a shadow of doubt, Louis, the Most Christian King of the French, whose kingdom it is considered never has
been defiled by schism, together with Henry, King of England, accepted Pope Alexander at the Lord's behest as the father and shepherd of their souls. The Kings of Spain, Sicily, Jerusalem, Hungary,
and the Emperor of the Greeks, with the patriarchs, bishops, princes
and all the clerks and people subject to them likewise did the same.
And so, while the whole world recognized the Roman Pontiff as the
Vicar of Christ and the Catholic successor of Blessed Peter, only the
aforesaid Emperor Frederick and his accomplices remained obdurate
and perverse in their error, vehemently assailing and eagerly persecuting Alexander and those prelates of the Churches who manfully
stood by him.

In the second year of his pontificate Pope Alexander returned to
Rome where, under the inspiration of God, he solemnly dedicated
the Church of Santa Maria Nuova. But since, because of the great
revolt of the schismatics, he could no longer remain at peace there,
he returned to Campagna, persuaded to do so by the requests of the
Romans. As the imperial persecution against the Church grew to
such an extent in and around about the City that the whole Patrimony of Peter from Acquapendente to Ceprano except the towns
of Orvieto, Terracina and Anagni and the fortress of Castro, had
been seized and placed under the rule of the Germans and schismatics, with the agreement of the loyal members of the Church,
Alexander decided to sail to France with his brethren. And so, after
appointing Julius, Bishop of Praeneste, as his Vicar in the City,
and arranging all other matters necessary for the good of the Church,
he journeyed to Terracina with his brethren, since from there he

intended to set sail. There he found four galleys which the King of Sicily had dispatched thither for his use, most beautifully appointed. Hardly had the court of the Pontiff and his brethren embarked with the necessary luggage than a strong and unexpected storm arose which made the calm sea a raging flood and drove the ships, overwhelmed by the crashing waves and the buffeting of the winds, against the rocks that lined the shore. There they were wrecked and broke up, though without loss of either life or possessions. Thus the voyage which the Pontiff had arranged for that time was delayed and obstacles were placed in its way.

But after a short interval of time the ships were repaired and the other things necessary for the voyage prepared, and within the octave of the Nativity, he with his brother Bishops, put out to sea from the promontory of Circei at the mouth of the river Olevola, and on the feast of St. Agnes, with the Lord as their helmsman, touched land at Genoa, where in spite of the prohibition of the persecutor of the Church, Frederick, he was received with all pomp and ceremony by all the clergy and layfolk. On Passion Sunday he set out from Genoa, sailed on in conditions as pleasant as one could wish for, and on Palm Sunday came to one of the Ligurian Islands, where the excessive roughness of the sea compelled him to celebrate Easter. On the following Wednesday he came to the church of Maguellone, where, inspired by God, he solemnly dedicated the high altar. But since the place itself was most unsuitable for the reception of guests and since a very great number of prelates of the church awaited the arrival of the Pontiff most affectionately but could not do so on the island, he considered it fitting to go up to the populous town of Montpellier. But when the white palfrey and the other customary pontifical insignia had been prepared, Pope Alexander could scarcely get his horse to go up on account of the great masses of people. He was hardly able to keep to the correct route. So great was the disgraceful and importunate mass of all who followed in his footprints that he who, with great effort, was able to touch so much as the hem of his cloak, considered himself lucky. William, the lord of the town, accompanied by his barons met him with military honours, and for the distance of a mile he performed the office of marshal. In a very great procession the Pontiff entered Montpellier. And there, among the other nobles who approached his path, was a certain loyal Saracen prince who reverently drew nigh with his entourage, and having kissed his feet, knelt before him and bowing his head worshipped

53

the Pontiff as if he were the holy and pious god of the Christians. He spoke to the Pontiff on behalf of a King of the Mahommedans who had sent him to those regions. He spoke respectfully in his own barbaric tongue and through an interpreter declared his entire meaning. The Pontiff answered him with kindness and in seriousness, and showed him very great honour, giving him a place at his feet among the others whom he had honoured. Seeing this, all who were in the presence of the Pontiff were very much surprised and recalled to one another the words of the prophet: 'All the kings of the earth shall adore him, and all nations shall serve him.'

When Sunday came, the Pontiff went to the principal church to celebrate the solemnities of the Mass. Since an immense crowd of men and women had gathered from all parts, after he had spoken to the people, Alexander gave a true account of his election and the insolent perfidy of the schismatics, and then solemnly renewed the sentence of excommunication laid on the persons of the heresiarch Octavian and the said Emperor Frederick and their accomplices.

At that time throughout Aquitaine and the neighbouring regions so great a famine was spreading that a number of men too great to be counted would surely die on account of the dearth of food. For this reason the French became greatly afraid lest a like affliction should enter their land.

The Pontiff, thinking it fitting that he should give notice of his arrival to the King of France, sent two of his brethren, namely, Bernard, Bishop of Ostia and J., Cardinal Deacon of St. Mary in Cosmidin as legates to that monarch, to learn his mind and to discover what districts of the Kingdom he would advise him to visit. The King received them with due ceremony out of veneration for the blessed Peter, treated them in an honourable manner, and after taking counsel sent them back with cheerful replies and great lightness of heart to their lord Alexander, whom he had already accepted as the father and shepherd of his soul. And so when they returned to the presence of their master and to the college of their brethren, and reported what the King had said to them in answer, all rejoiced. The Pontiff therefore left Montpellier in the next month, June, and travelling through Alès, Mende and Le Puy, he came to Auvergne, and on the Vigil of the Assumption of the Blessed Virgin arrived happily, with God's help, in Clermont Ferrand. In the meantime, Frederick, seeing the whole world run after Alexander and that the Kings and Princes of orthodox faith

54

throughout the world showed him the honour and reverence due to a Roman Pontiff, was consumed with envy, confused and terrified by the accusations of his conscience. For he was ashamed to desist from the evil he had put in train, since he was more brave and more powerful than his predecessors, and had already placed under his yoke almost the whole of Italy. Moreover, he was exceedingly hesitant and fearful for the loss of the imperial crown, should Alexander prevail in his days. Placed therefore in a hazard of such great uncertainty, he took counsel within himself, worldly-wise, sagacious and clever, how to cast down Alexander and his own idol at one and the same time, by a judgement of the Church and raise a third person to the Roman Pontificate. And since everyone has a natural desire to unite to himself others like-minded, he summoned Count Henry of Troyes, in whom he had the greatest trust. He revealed to him his thoughts, won him over to his opinion, and made him an assistant and co-worker for his plan. The Count, at the behest of the Emperor, who had given him instructions to do so, returned to his own country, and approached, like the Tempter his Lord, the King of France, a man pious but having the simplicity of a dove. With cunning and deceit he suggested to him, on behalf of the Emperor, an allegedly desirable plan for restoring the peace of the Roman Church. 'The Emperor', Henry said, 'from his contemplation on the Divine Love, wishes to perform this good work with you in this way: the two of you, the two greatest Princes of the world, are to meet at Dijon on the boundary between your Kingdom and his Empire, with the principal persons, both clerical and lay, of the Empire and your Kingdom. He himself will bring with him Octavian with his followers, and you are to have with you Alexander with his court. After you and your parties are assembled, in the presence of so many personages, the reports of the election of each shall be diligently heard and examined. Then, by the Churches of France, Italy, and Germany gathered there, let decree be made concerning each of the two as seems best, and let the affairs of the Church of Rome be decided and settled in whatever way seems best and most useful'. This idea for the restoration of peace to the Church appeared a good one to the King, a true Israelite in whom there was no guile. Since because of the discord, very many evils were growing in all the churches, in his simplicity of heart he succumbed to the blandishments of the Count and allowed him to grant surety in his name to the Emperor concerning the matters which had been suggested to him. The Count therefore, happy at succeeding in gaining what he had asked for, returned from the French court to the Emperor who was at that time in Lombardy, and took an oath on the part of his lord the King, as we have described above. These evil tidings spread through all the provinces of Italy and France, and Catholics would have been full of grief and fear at what had been done had the Lord not brought to naught that plot against the ancient liberty of the Church.

On the day appointed, the Emperor Frederick came to Dijon with a large number of princes and men-at-arms, together with Octavian and his crew of accomplices in his train. The King of the French with his Archbishops and Bishops as well as his barons was also drawing near to the same place, when he met Pope Alexander at Souvigny. Here they remained two days, showing each other due honour, with the purpose of setting out for the colloquy together. But since it was quite unworthy and contrary to the statutes of the holy Fathers that the Supreme Pontiff and the First See should have to submit to human judgement, all considered appropriate that only some of the more important personages of the Roman Church should accompany the King to Dijon in order to prove that the election of their Lord Alexander was canonical and just, and that as a result the subsequent actions of Octavian were invalid. From the Pontiff went as legates B., Bishop of Porto; Hu., of the title of Santa Croce; I., Cardinal Priest of the title of Santa Anastasia; I., Cardinal Deacon of Santa Maria in Cosmidin; and A., Cardinal Deacon of San Teodoro. They accompanied the King of the French to Dijon. After their departure the Pontiff, with his remaining brother Bishops, turned aside to the abbey of Déols in Aquitaine.

The King, accompanied by many persons of great importance, after he arrived at Dijon, went forward as far as the middle of the bridge over the Saône, the river that divides Germany from France, awaiting the Emperor's proposals for the Church. The heresiarch Octavian, seeing that the more important personages of the Church of Rome had come with the Church of France to oppose him and that they were most firmly opposed to him, became exceedingly afraid and began to lose all hope about what he had done. He therefore turned to the Emperor and said to him: 'Since that opponent of mine has disdained to come hither, do you allow my cause, which was judged in your presence and approved at the Council of Lodi, to be once again judged and dealt with?' Then the Emperor, noticing that the countenance of Octavian himself was very troubled, pretended to be moved to anger against the King of the French and addressed him through his representatives thus: 'See, you apparently have already deceived me, and clearly have come in a manner contrary to the oath of the colloquy, since you have not brought with you that Pope of yours as you had promised'. The King took counsel and answered him in this fashion: 'Although I am able to excuse the absence of the Pontiff in a just and reasonable way, yet so that no-one may say anything derogatory on any point to the honour of the Kingdom entrusted to me and of my reputation, and so that I may not incur justly or unjustly a reputation for deceit, I shall summon the Pontiff himself with his Bishops without delay, and without deceit and fraud, to this place, and make him come'. And so the King, as he had promised, urgently despatched trusty messengers to Alexander, bidding him to come to him with his brethren without delay unless he wished the King to be detained in the Emperor's custody, for this had been the decision taken between them. When they heard this the Pontiff and his brothers, being of the opinion that the King of the French had been deceitfully ensnared, grew most anxious and, looking ahead to the very great dangers that threatened on every side, they were very much afraid. For they saw that if they were to go forward with the intention of submitting themselves to the judgement of men, violence would bring danger to the liberty of the Church; but if they were not to go, a sure seizure of their persons and the despoiling of their goods seemed to be imminent because of the arrest of the King. In truth the Emperor's very great power was frightening and very much to be feared; it was believed he had brought to Dijon the Kings of Denmark and Bohemia with his own dukes and princes, and also a large host of armed soldiers to bring to fruition in that colloquy the plans that he had already harboured for the detriment of the Pontiff and the King of the French.

But the good and merciful Lord, Who does not abandon those that have hope in Him, and brings to naught the wicked counsels of princes, did not allow the Pontiff and the pious King of the French to be more tried than they could bear in such straits. In an unhoped for way He solved the issue which had been such a temptation for them. He aroused the glorious King of England to come in haste, fired with a great anger, to assist and support his lord, the King of the French, with a very large host of mighty warriors against the same Emperor. He brought so great a scourge of famine upon the Emperor's army, that on account of the very great dearth, hungry men paid a silver mark for a loaf of average size. The Emperor, because he could neither remain there nor carry out the plans he had fomented, quickly sought to find as honourable an opportunity as he could of withdrawing. He therefore addressed these words to the most excellent King of the French through his Chancellor Rainald and through others of his cause: 'Our master Frederick, Emperor of the Romans and special Patron of the Church of Rome, bids you remember that it belongs to no prelate of the Church to give judgement concerning the matter of the election of the Roman Pontiff. Judgement is reserved to the men of the Holy Roman Empire. Therefore, it seems right and just that you ought to go to the Emperor as to a friend with your Bishops and clergy, and to hear the opinions of such people.' When he heard this, the King, allowing himself a little smile, answered them in this way: 'I am surprised that so cunning a man has sent to me words so untruthful and untrustworthy. Does he not know that our Lord Jesus Christ, when He was on earth, entrusted to the blessed Peter and through Him to his successors, the pasturing of His flock? Has he not heard in the Gospel that it was said by the same Son of God to the Prince of the Apostles: "If you love me, Peter, feed my sheep"? Surely the Kings of the French and certain prelates of the churches are not excepted here? Or are the Bishops of my Kingdom not of the sheep which the Son of God entrusted to Peter?' When he had said this he turned his horse away in contempt for them, and straightway taking up arms, as did his barons and the rest of his army, he strengthened the weak points of his kingdom. Like a strong and prudent man, he returned to his capital with glory and honour under the merciful bounty of the Lord. The brethren who had been sent by the Pontiff to the King returned joyfully and recounted all that had happened at the colloquy for the honour of God and the Church through the hard work of the glorious and orthodox King. For this reason the College of Bishops and all who were present gave thanks with rejoicing and exultation to the Lord Jesus Christ Who had dealt mercifully with them and had deigned to set them free from the hands of a most powerful enemy. But the Emperor, shamefaced, was forced by the great want caused by the famine to dismiss his army to their homes, while he himself returned to Germany with no little sadness.

It was at that time that the King of England in person paid a visit to his lord, Pope Alexander, at the monastery of Déols to prostrate himself humbly at his feet, and to be received in the embrace of the same Pontiff after kissing his foot and offering gifts of gold. He subsequently declined to sit on the faldstool prepared for him, but desired to sit with his barons on the ground at the feet of the Pontiff. After the space of three days, greatly gladdened by the pleasant countenance of the Pontiff, and when he and his brethren had had magnificent gifts bestowed upon them, he withdrew from the Papal presence.

The Pontiff, having dedicated the High Altar of the abbey of Déols, continued his journey to Tours, and arrived with all good fortune by the Lord's help about the feast of St. Michael. There he made a stay for some time and celebrated the Nativity of the Lord with due ceremony. When Lent came, he went on to Paris with the intention of holding discussions about various matters. But before he could enter Paris, the King, like the meek and pious man that he was, met him with his barons and soldiery at a distance of two leagues from the city. The King, when he came in sight of the Pope, immediately got down from his mount, and hastening to the Pope's litter, humbly kissed his feet, and was immediately received into his embrace. Then going forward together with all despatch, they entered Paris. The clergy in a long and seemly procession met the Pope and led him with gladness and rejoicing to the principal church. In that city he remained the whole of Lent, and there celebrated the feast of Easter. And since the octave of Pentecost, for which he had summoned a Council at Tours, was drawing close, he left Paris and returned quickly there by way of Chartres.

In the year of the Incarnation of the Lord 1163, the eleventh of the indiction, and the fourth of his pontificate, on 19 May, Pope Alexander solemnly opened his Council in the Church of St. Maurice at Tours. In attendance upon him were seventeen Cardinals, 124 Bishops and 414 abbots, and a very large number of other persons both clerical and lay. At this Council the Apostolic Constitutions were in due course reaffirmed, and these new chapters promulgated:

While the greater benefices of the Church remain whole and entire, it seems particularly unsuitable that the lesser ones should be divided. For this reason, that the Church may possess unity in its least members as much as in its greatest, we forbid the division of prebends or the transfer of dignities.

A large number of the clergy, and, as we have learnt to our grief, of those also who by their profession and dress have withdrawn from the world, while abhorring almost too clearly the common forms of usury, take as pledge the estates of those in need whom they have assisted with money, and receive from them the income that is not their due. Wherefore, by the authority of a General Council we decree that from this day forth no-one who has been raised to the rank of clerk may presume to benefit by this or by any other kind of usury. And if anyone has previously taken the property of any person as pledge with an expectation of this nature, and after calculation of his expenses has already received what is his due by a deduction from the income, let him restore possession in full to the debtor. But if he has received anything less, let possession be freely restored to the owner when he has what is due to him. But if after the promulgation of the Constitutions of this Synod there is anyone among the clergy who insists on his abominable profits from the practice of usury, let him suffer the loss of his ecclesiastical office. We except only the case of a benefice of the Church which a cleric may redeem in this way from lay hands.

Though it is considered an exceedingly grave matter, and one worthy of divine judgement, that certain lay persons usurp in the affairs of the Church what belongs to the priestly office, it strikes greater dread and grief in our heart that it is very often said that the cause of their wrongdoing is in God Himself. For certain ones among our brethren and fellow Bishops and other prelates of the Church themselves bestow upon them the tithes and revenues of the Church and thereby drive off into the byways of death those who ought to be recalled by their preaching to the way of life. Of such persons God speaks through the prophet: 'The sins of my people devour them and provoke their souls to iniquities'. Wherefore we decree that if anyone make a gift of a church or a tithe to any layman who remains in the world, he is to be cut down from his place like the tree that uselessly encumbers the ground, and to lie prostrate in his suffering until he makes good the damage that he has done.

In the districts about Toulouse a damnable heresy has even now appeared, which like a cancer is gradually spreading to places round about and has already infected Gascony and very many other provinces. While it hides like a snake beneath its own coils and the more silently it creeps about the more serious is the ruin it brings among simple folk to the cause of the Lord. Wherefore we urge all Bishops and priests of the Lord who dwell in those parts to watch against this heresy, and under pain of excommunication to forbid anyone, when the followers of that heresy have been recognized, to grant them refuge in his lands or offer them assistance. Not even in buying and selling should consort be had with them, so that when at length the support of men has been lost to them, they may be forced to return to their senses from the error of their ways. And if anyone attempts to resist these decrees let him be anathematized as one who has a share in their iniquity.

And if Catholic princes seize heretics of this sort, let them consign them to prison and punish them with the loss of all their goods. And since the heretics frequently gather together from various districts into one lair, and have, other than a common error, no reason for living together and yet dwell in a single dwelling, let such conventicles be keenly sought out and when they are discovered let them be forbidden with the severity of the canons.

Since a certain monstrous custom has grown up in certain localities in opposition to the decrees of the holy Fathers, of appointing priests to the service of the churches for an annual salary, this we forbid absolutely; for when the office of priest is disposed of by bargaining, no consideration is had for the penalty of eternal punishment.

Avarice is not reduced among the people to any useful extent if it is not guarded against by those who are enrolled among the ranks of the clergy, and especially by those who spurning the world profess the name and discipline of religion. We therefore forbid that any payment should be demanded from those who wish to transfer to the religious life, that any office of prior or chaplaincy whatsoever among monks or clerks should be offered annually for sale, or that any fee should be required of those to whom the service of such offices is entrusted. The authority of the holy Fathers clearly states that this is simoniacal. Wherefore, let anyone who presumes to attempt to do this, either him that gives or him that takes, have no doubt but that he will have his portion with Simon. Let no-one moreover demand a fee for burial or for the reception of chrism and the holy oil, nor is anyone to disclaim guilt under the plea of some ancient custom, because usage increases rather than lessens sin.

Since in certain sees some Deans or Archpriests are appointed for an annual consideration to perform the duties of Bishops or Archdeacons and to determine ecclesiastical cases, and since this without doubt leads to distress among priests and to the subversion of justice, we place this practice under a most serious ban. And if anyone continues this practice he is to be removed from the ranks of the clergy. Let the Bishop, moreover, who continues this practice in his See or allows the judgements of the church courts to be subverted by means of deceit, suffer the punishment prescribed by the canons.

Without arduous efforts on our part the ancient Enemy brings low in his envy the weak members of the Church. But he also lays his hands upon its preferred members and strives to overthrow every chosen one, for, as Scripture says: 'They are his chosen meats'. He considers that he has brought about the ruin of many whenever one of the more precious members of the Church has been pulled down by his wiles. For this

61

reason it is not to be marvelled at that, transforming himself, as is his custom, into an angel of light, under the pretext of showing concern for the bodies of those members who are languishing under their burdens and of negotiating in a more trustworthy way the business of the Church, he entices those who are under monastic rule to read law and weigh out prescriptions. Wherefore, that spiritual men may not be involved once more in the affairs of the world under the pretext of learning, and in interior matters fail in that very concern which they think to have for others in external needs, with the consent of the Council gathered in this place we decree that no one at all after profession of the vows of religion is allowed to depart to read medicine or civil law. Should he however depart and not return to his cloister within the space of two months, he is to be shunned by all as excommunicate, and, should he attempt to appear as counsel in a case he is not to be heard. If he returns to his choir, chapter, board, and the rest, he is always to be the least of the brethren, and is to lose all hope of advancement except by favour of the Apostolic See.

And we render null and void the regulations made by Octavian and other schismatics and heretics.

At the end of the Council, Pope Alexander received a message from the Kings of France and England to the effect that if he wished to make his residence for a long period in some part of their Kingdoms, he was to choose according to his good pleasure some town or city which pleased him. For this reason, when the Council was over he travelled to the city of Sens, intending to make his residence there in that metropolitan city because it lay in a fertile district, and was easy of access for visitors. In this place he made a long stay from the 1 October 1163 to the Easter of 1165, and in the business of the Catholic Church he showed the care and diligence due to his office.

At the same time the heresiarch Octavian of unhappy memory fell ill at Lucca, where about the feast of Easter he, still unrepentant and excommunicate, went forth from this world to the place below. It is affirmed by some that he summoned a Catholic priest to his bedside, who could not go in to him however as he was prevented by the schismatics. Imar, who had formerly been Bishop of Tusculum, and who was one of his chief allies, a person whom we have spoken of in an earlier place, scarcely outlived the frightful day of his master's death, and met his own wretched end at Cluny. Now there remained only two of the four false brethren who had abandoned the unity of the Church to the ruin of their souls—two smouldering members, John of St. Martin and Guy of Crema, who were afflicted with tears and grief. Trembling not a little where there was no fear, the one said to the other: 'If we choose to be reconciled to Alexander, perhaps he will receive us only with intolerable reproaches and to our everlasting confusion. But if he will receive us, perhaps he will do to us afterwards what Pope Innocent did to those Cardinals who took sides against him with Peter de Leone'. Lacking hope of being received by the Church, they called together the rest of the schismatics, both clerical and lay, who had gathered from Italy and Germany for the burial of Octavian. When they had all assembled in one place, like the stubborn and faithless men they were, they raised over themselves Guy of Crema as another idol, and bowing down before his feet they worshipped him. Straightway they sent in haste to the Emperor, who was at that time in Germany, to seek confirmation from the imperial authority for their abominable deed and asked for speedy assistance by the power of his help through imperial letters and honoured messengers that they might not be brought to naught by Alexander.

When the Emperor had certain report of the death of Octavian, he was deeply saddened and sorrowful; and so that he should not seem to be defeated and overcome in his evil proposal, without delay he put behind him all fear of God and agreed to so great an evil. He made it his task to give fresh life as far as he could to a schism that had already been quenched. For the increase of his own damnation, for putting great fear among Catholics and for making his accomplices stronger in their evil doing, he added sin to sin by an oath made with his own lips and with his hand on the holy Gospels that he would always consider Guy and his successors as Catholics, and Alexander and his successors as schismatics. He also forced such churchmen as he could ensnare to swear the same oath. In this execrable deed, what did he try to achieve other than the division of the Church of Christ? For as the Creed tells us, each Catholic Christian believes not in two but in one Holy Catholic and Apostolic Church, and so on each Sunday does he sing and affirm. For this reason we find in another part of the Scriptures: 'My dove is one, my perfect one, the only daughter of her mother, the chosen one of her that bore her'. The blessed Apostle Paul teaches this unity of the Church and demonstrates the sacrament of unity, when he writes: 'One body and one spirit, one hope of our calling, one Lord, one Faith, one Baptism, one God'. Does the Emperor Frederick, who does not believe in this unity, believe that he holds to the faith? He who abandons the Chair of Peter which is the foundation of the Church, how can he trust to be in the Church? For as he who was outside the Ark of Noah could not escape his doom, there is no way in which he who is outside the Church can escape his.

Moreover, we ought to recall that before the Emperor went to the colloquy with the King of the French, after the destruction of Tortona, Milan and Crema, he had imposed so heavy a burden of servitude on the whole of Lombardy as not only to take away their possessions by force, but also by his minions to lay hands on wives and daughters and brazenly to dishonour them without risk of punishment—a thing that is not allowed among pagans without payment of the ultimate penalty. On account of these and other insupportable wrongs, Venice, Verona, Padua, Vicenza, and the whole of the March that bordered them, secretly came together and held long consultations on this heavy burden of oppression. At length they all swore that, saving the right of the old Empire, they would do nothing more for the Emperor than what it is agreed had been required by his predecessors of old, Charlemagne that is and the other orthodox Emperors. Having without exception made an alliance and having bound themselves with the ties of an oath, they undertook little by little to fortify their towns, to put down the haughty dealings of the Germans, and to take the offensive more vigorously against those whom they found in rebellion against themselves.

When this came to the ears of the Emperor, his anger was inflamed, and straightway gathering an army, in concert with Pavia and Cremona and the rest of the Lombards whom he thought trustworthy, he advanced to do battle against Verona. The League of Verona, with full confidence in the justice of their cause, came forth boldly from their city with a great host of armed men, and coolly pitched their tents not far from the pavilions of their opponents. But when on both sides they stood ready to commence battle, the Emperor realized that the Lombards who had accompanied him were for his opponents. His fear was great, and in shame and great confusion he broke camp, and instead of giving battle, turned tail and fled.

From that time on he held all the cities of Italy in suspicion, and sought to be feared rather than loved by them. From this it came about that on the advice of his Markgraves, Counts, and Captains, who were held in hatred by the cities, he took in hand the building of impregnable citadels and other strong defences, and had them held and closely guarded by the more trustworthy sort of Germans. He appointed Germans as lords and masters over Lombardy and Tuscany, so that no Italian might have any position at all from which to resist his will. Having arranged all these matters and appointed them according to his good pleasure, he went off to his conference with the King of the French, which we have already described, and from there returned to Germany.

Matters being as they now were, when the cities of Lombardy of which the names are found below, discovered from such indications the entirely harsh and evil intention and plan of the Emperor against themselves, they could discover no other sure way of escaping their fate than that all should make a firm stand with the city of Verona against every man for the protection of their freedom, and, giving one another equal aid, should grant each other support and all needed assistance. These cities were in league with Verona: in the first place Cremona, then the people of Milan, who had been settled by the Emperor outside the ruins of their city, Piacenza also, Brescia, and Bergamo. Swiftly the alliance grew very large, and became both firm and strong. The other cities of Italy, seeing this, rejoiced inwardly, and though they outwardly obeyed for fear of the Emperor, inwardly they were heart and soul for the cities of the League.

It was while circumstances were in this state that Julius, Bishop of Praeneste, Pope Alexander's Vicar, died, and I. Cardinal Priest of SS. John and Paul was appointed in his stead. At his behest, the people of Rome for the most part swore the customary oath of fealty to Pope Alexander, a large sum of money having been handed over on his behalf to them. He appointed a Senate by choosing new members according to his will and pleasure. This Senate restored to the new Vicar the Sabine county and the Church of St. Peter, which since the Emperor's violent seizure was at that time held by schismatics. So it came about that almost the whole of the city was held by the Vicar for the glory and use of Pope Alexander. The Vicar took counsel with faithful members of the Church, both lay and clerical, about recalling the Pope to the See of St. Peter and the Lateran Palace, and sent both legates and letters to Pope Alexander at Sens in France, begging and praying him on behalf of the whole clergy and people of Rome, and of all those faithful to him, that he should deign to return to his own See and to the people most especially entrusted to him. 'Primacy and government in the Church has been given to this City by none other than the Lord Himself, so that the City which in the ages of paganism was more glorious than all others, should by divine mandate have in the age of the Christian revelation a magisterial dignity above all others. Though many have attempted to resist this divine disposition and kick against it with their heels, through the protection of God none has been able to prevail. Since in this matter we have asked the opinion in a healthy spirit not only of ourselves but of all the Churches and people of Italy, most dear Father and Lord, this course is necessary. They all hope that your return to the City and your taking repossession of the Chair of Blessed Peter may, under the guidance of God, result in peace for themselves and quiet for the whole world.

When he had heard and pondered this message, the Pontiff held wide-ranging discussions concerning his return to the City with Bishops and Cardinals, because he foresaw that many serious and difficult matters were hanging over him. But after taking the advice of the Kings of France and England as well as of the Bishops of France, he gave firm answer to his Vicar about his return, and straightway hastened to equip himself for the journey.

Having celebrated the holy feast of Easter, he left Sens, and journeying by Paris, Bourges, and Le Puy, he arrived safely, through divine favour, at Montpellier after the feast of the Apostles. When the ships and everything else considered necessary for sailing had been prepared, he embarked with his brethren during the octave of the Assumption, and traversing the immense deep of the sea not without much difficulty, drawn by well-filled sails he touched land at the city of Messina. When this news reached the ears of William, the most Christian King of Sicily, at Palermo, a monarch whose memory we ought to recall, he recognized the same Pontiff as the father and lord from whom his inheritance of Sicily and all his other lands were held, and ordered him to be treated with due honour and be presented with great gifts. A red galley was to be prepared also with the greatest care for carrying his venerable person, and four for the use of the Bishops and Cardinals. He appointed the Archbishop of Reggio and other great men to accompany the Pontiff in honour and attend him in splendour and bring him to the city of Rome with pomp and ceremony.

Pope Alexander left Messina in November and passing by Salerno and Gaeta, with the assistance of the prayers of the blessed Apostles

66

Peter and Paul, entered the mouth of the Tiber on the feast of St. Cecilia and arrived by divine guidance at Ostia where he rested that night in safety and good health with his brethren. When morning came the Senate and nobility and a great crowd of clergy and people came out of the City to meet him with all reverence, displaying to him as to the shepherd of their souls all due and customary veneration. From there they conducted him with all due ceremony in gladness and rejoicing and with olive branches to the Lateran Gate. There the whole body of the clergy, dressed in the vestments customary for a solemn feast, awaited the arrival of the Pontiff desired for so long. Thither came the Jews, bearing, as was their custom, the law in their hands and thither came the ensigns with their standards, the marshals, the keepers of the caskets, the judges with their advocates and an extraordinary gathering of the people. A procession was formed with due reverence. From all sides there rose the sound of sweet voices, and the Pope was led with such pomp and exultation to the patriarchal church of the Holy Saviour and the Lateran Palace as none remembers to have been extended to a Roman Pontiff for many a long year.

These things were done in the year of the Incarnation of the Lord 1165, the thirteenth indication, on 23 November, and in the sixth year of his Pontificate.

While these things were happening in the city of Rome, and Pope Alexander was sitting as Christ's Vicar in the Chair of blessed Peter, Guy of Crema and his accomplices were very troubled and confused, for fear and trembling had seized them. But the Catholics, though they underwent many sufferings at the hands of the Emperor Frederick, were gladdened by the favourable turn of events for the Church and by the great confusion of the schismatics. The Lombard League remained steadfast against the Church's enemies and against those who were attacking their liberty. They arranged everything they considered useful to their defence, and to bring to naught the plots and machinations prepared by the Emperor for their destruction, they shunned no toil and diligence for the sake of strength. So it happened that the citizens of Verona and Padua, like warlike men and lovers of liberty, caused serious interruption to the Emperor's advance through their own territories. For the protection of their own territories, they attacked the heavily fortified castle of Rivoli and its outlying citadel with a strong force. They stormed them bravely and razed them.

67

At that time the Emperor collected an army and for the third time invaded Lombardy unexpectedly and, making his way through the Val Camonica, encamped in the territory of Brescia. Although he held the cities of Lombardy in loathing and placed no trust in them, since they had all taken the field against him together, yet it was not safe to cause them any injury or harm. He therefore dissimulated the savagery he felt in his heart towards them, and appeared kind and cheerful towards them. As in customary when so great a prince appears, nobles and townsfolk came together before him and showed to him due and customary honour. He advanced therefore towards Ferrara, and then in all tranquility moved close to Bologna, where he arranged to stay on account of sickness in his army. In the meantime he ordered some of his chief men with soldiers to advance into Tuscany to give support and strength to Guy of Crema, whom once more he had set up like an idol against God, zealous in bringing troubles and injuries upon Pope Alexander and the Romans. He himself descended with his army upon Ancona. Because the Emperor of the Greeks having seized Ancona by force held that city by the distribution of an immense sum of money among the citizens, Frederick laid siege to it and strove with all his might to take it by storm in order to avenge the insult offered to his person and rule. Furthermore, the savagery which he had released upon Tuscany as a result of the disputes and wars which had arisen between Pisa and Lucca so terrified all men and made them submit to the Emperor's yoke that in the Roman dominions there was scarcely anyone who dared resist the Emperor's commands. Then the towns which lay around Rome and their captains were beset by Germans and forced to abandon their usual loyalty and subjection to blessed Peter. And so these criminals laid waste the whole land with looting, arson, and other infamies.

Since they could not subject Rome, the mother of cities, to the Emperor by force of arms, they hoped and indeed attempted to corrupt it by the distribution of sums of money. And because Rome would put herself up for sale if it could find a buyer, as one of the ancient writers said, there was no lack of Romans who having taken the money made so bold as to defy all opinion and swear fealty to the heresiarch Guy and the Emperor. And so, since these serious evils were growing on every hand, the kind Pontiff frequently rebuked his people with a fatherly affection, begging them to be of one opinion with himself and the Church, to call back to their

68

allegiance the neighbouring cities and their captains and bind them in alliance to themselves. He also warned them to stand shoulder to shoulder in the defence of City and Church against a most powerful enemy. He even offered the money of the Church to the people for them to spend on defence for the benefit of the Church. But their attachment to their sins was so great that he could do nothing with his people, who pretended to be for each side, yet did not side loyally with either. Since the people neither gave heed to the voice of their shepherd nor took precautions against the disasters that were coming upon them, they rightly fell under the vengeance of God, since they deserved the loss both of lives and possessions.

At that time, when the Emperor Frederick was still laying siege to Ancona, the Lombard League, greatly strengthened in the solidity of their freedom, considered it worthwhile to restore, with the aid of the Lord, the Milanese to their city and to rebuild the walls which had been razed. They were all the more eager because they recalled the merits of Blessed Ambrose. To give a greater permanence to their enterprise, the League joined Lodi and the Milanese by a treaty of friendship, and bound them by the tie of a closer affection. The former city had indeed been recently transferred to a strongly fortified site by the Emperor to be a thorn in the side of other cities. The League drove out the schismatics and the imposed officials and appointed Bishops and other prelates of the Church, in every city and see, a task in which they were assisted by the Lord. Although the Emperor was saddened to his very core by these events, he chose to appear to tolerate them for the time being rather than to make his cause, which at that very moment was poised on a knife's edge, worse.

At this juncture the loyal and devout child of the Church of Rome, William, illustrious and glorious King of Sicily, died peacefully at Palermo. His soul we recommended to the Lord. His elder son, also named William, succeeded to his Kingdom and to his loyalty and devotion.

At the same time, Manuel, the great and mighty Emperor of Constantinople, learning of the insults and injuries which the Emperor Frederick was attempting to inflict on the venerable Pope Alexander in opposition both to God and every form of justice, sent to Rome his Imperial *Sebastus*, Jordan, to aid and serve the Pontiff. Jordan was the son of that Robert who had been Prince of Capua. When the *Sebastus* came, he bowed down low before the Pontiff, and at his feet offered great and precious gifts, and with grave manner revealed the instructions which he had received. Now among the instructions there appeared one in particular which seemed acceptable both to God and to men. For he declared that the Emperor wished to make the Greek Church one with the mother of all Churches, the sacred Church of Rome, just as it had been in the better days gone by, so that by a single observance of the law of God, and under a single Head of the Church, the clergy and people of both traditions, Latin as well as Greek, might live in a unity that would never end. Nor was that all: the Emperor asked that since the occasion was just and a favourable and opportune moment had offered itself, the crown of the Roman Empire should be restored to him by the Apostolic See, since, he declared, it belonged to him by right and not to that German, Frederick. He solemnly engaged himself, in order to bring this task to a successful conclusion, to spend such a fortune in silver and gold and the strength of brave men that there could be no doubt that not only Rome but also the whole of Italy would return to the service of the Church, if the Emperor would have his crown restored to him. Since the message appeared extremely complex and needed much consideration, it seemed useful to the Pontiff, after he had heard the opinions of his brethren and of the more trusty men of the City itself, to send the Bishop of Ostia and the Cardinal of SS. John and Paul as legates *a latere* with the *Sebastus* to the Emperor's court to treat of his case.

In the seventh year of his pontificate, the Roman people aroused among others the hatred of the neighbouring cities of Alba and Tusculum. On account of the pressing evil of the time, these cities had taken the part of the Germans, and on account of the heaviness of the exactions demanded by the latter they were not paying their tribute to Rome. Since rivalry grew among the towns, the Roman people, in the month of May, when the harvest was growing white and despite the prohibition of their Shepherd, went out under arms with a bold show against Raino, lord of Tusculum. The Romans advanced into his territory and in their enmity not only laid waste vines and crops but also strove to destroy the walls of Tusculum. Since Raino could not resist so great a force nor protect his land, he had of necessity to turn to the Emperor for help. And so the Emperor sent quickly to the aid and defence of Raino a large host of brave warriors, to protect the people of Tusculum and check the insolence of the Romans. When those Germans savages, accustomed to war, reached Tusculum and saw that the Romans, while strong in numbers, were weak in disposition, they took heart and were encouraged to do battle with them on the plain without delay. The two armies met in the afternoon and all of a sudden a loud cry rose to the heavens from either side. Drawing their swords, enemy rushed upon enemy most fiercely. But at the first onset, the Romans crumpled and in the plains as well as among pathless precipices were so harried until nightfall and so cut down that barely a third of their great army escaped. On that night there arose throughout the whole city a sudden grief and a great wailing. The disaster was unprecedented, the mourning such that it would not be stilled, the overthrow of men and their goods beyond repair. Nay, from the day when Hannibal had defeated the Romans at Cannae no one could recall such a defeat of Roman arms. But although in such great grief and universal sorrow the Pontiff could nowise restrain himself from weeping and tears, yet when he saw the city bereft of the protection of both arms and men-of-war, he quickly mounted a watchful guard over the city, undertook the repair of weakened portions of the walls, and then sought help from outside.

Overjoyed at the victory they had gained, the enemy were not contented with it, but uniting with the people of Tivoli, Alba Longa and Campagna, and other cities that lie close by, they advanced in haste from Tusculum to Rome. They destroyed all the defence works and all the crops as far as the Tiber, then surrounded the city up to its gates. The Emperor too, when he learnt of the great slaughter of Romans, left Ancona, and coming to his army, encamped with a great host on Monte Mario on July 19. On the next day, putting his trust in the large host he had gathered together, he advanced to the attack with a powerful force against the gates of the castle of Sant' Angelo. There he made a most ferocious assault with frequent attacks. But because the household of the supreme Pontiff, which is known under another name as his manse, in the face of these attacks, through the intercession of Blessed Peter, resisted bravely and manfully, he gained nothing on that day but the loss of men and the disgrace of defeat. For this reason, moved to greater fury, he made a violent attack with artillery and archers on the Church of the Prince of the Apostles, which was being guarded by persons faithful to the Church. When he was unable to take it by storm, putting aside all fear of God and of the Keeper of the Keys

71

of the Kingdom of Heaven, like the sacrilegious and profane man that he was, he had it set on fire. But the guardians of the Basilica, afraid lest the whole fabric of the Church might be destroyed by fire, after Santa Maria nella Torre with its brazen doors and the neighbouring colonnades had been consumed by the flames, surrendered it into the hands and power of the bloodthirsty monarch.

The blessed Pontiff had had anxious forebodings of imminent disasters. After that slaughter of the people which had happened as a result of their sins, he quitted the Lateran Palace and went with his brother Bishops and their households to the Palace of the Frangipani, which was a secure house. They retired in safety to Santa Maria Nuova, to the Torre Cartularia and the Colosseum, and there, on account of the malice of the Emperor that hung over them, was held a daily meeting of Bishops and Cardinals. Business was transacted and replies given.

At the same time, the King of Sicily, learning that that fierce persecutor of the Church was besieging Rome, and fearing lest something more serious should befall the person of his Lord Pope Alexander, sent to him two fast galleys with a large sum of money, bidding the captains to do their utmost to reach the Pope, and, having handed over to him the money, to take him and his brother Bishops aboard and rescue him from the power of Frederick and from the plots of the schismatics. It happened unexpectedly that the galleys sailed up the Tiber without challenge and touched shore close to the Church of St. Paul. A secret message was sent to the Supreme Pontiff and conducted by that excellent man Odo Frangipani, the captains of the galleys came to him with the money that they carried. Then the venerable Pontiff giving thanks to God Almighty for this turn of events, received the money with good wishes, and, in fatherly affection, kept the messengers of so devoted a prince in his company for a week. He took counsel about the affairs of the City and the Church, and then sent back the galleys with thanks to the King, the most devoted and special son of Blessed Peter, sending with them two of his brother Bishops, Manfred of San Giorgio and Peter of Santa Maria in Aciro, both Cardinal Deacons, to San Germano. Of the money which he had received he gave a part to those faithful servants of the Church, the Frangipani and the sons of Peter de Leone, binding them thus more closely to each other and making sure they would assist each other all the more, and support the people in the defence of the city and give them greater

72

encouragement. He also sent part of the money with fatherly kindness to the people of each of the gates for their defence of the City.

Now since the citizens of Rome were withstanding Frederick with a greater bravery than usual, and were daily inflicting upon him quite serious losses, he saw that he could not prevail against them by force of arms, and like a crafty fox he fell back upon his accustomed arguments and his penetrating cunning. Words of peace were sent to the Bishops and Cardinals through the mouth of Archbishop Conrad of Mainz, who by leave of Pope Alexander had gone to the Emperor: 'If you bring it about that without invalidating any one decree of his, he resigns the papacy, I will cause Guy of Crema to resign. Then let all the prelates of the Church gather together at one time, to elect some third person as Supreme Pontiff. I will restore to the Church a secure peace and shall never more concern myself in the matter of the choice of the Roman Pontiff.' He promised, moreover, that in return, he would restore to the Roman people all his prisoners of war and whatever remained of the spoils taken by his Germans. This word was so agreeable to the people that they unanimously recommended that this should be done. For they said that to redeem his sheep the Lord Pope ought to do even greater things than abdicate the papacy. But the Bishops and Cardinals, after deliberating, made this most vigorous reply to Frederick himself: 'It is not our duty to judge the Supreme Pontiff whom God has reserved for His own judgement, since, as the Scriptures assert, "the disciple is not above his master" '.

Since, however, the people strongly pressed the Pontiff to give effect to Frederick's request, Alexander, having a regard for what would be more beneficial to the Church, discussed the situation in secret with a few of his brother Bishops, and then disappeared from sight. But, under God's merciful dispensation, three days later, he was seen dining with his companions at the foot of Monte Circello, at the spring which since that time has been called the Spring of the Pope. Crossing the river Legula and with crowds of persons both lay and clerical coming to meet him from every quarter, he passed through Terracina and Gaeta with rejoicing and gladness, and at last through the Lord's favour, arrived with a host of Bishops at his patrimony of Benevento. His brothers who had remained in the City after his departure followed in his footsteps and remained attached to their head like limbs to their body.

73

But Frederick, when he discovered that the Pope, by leaving the City, had escaped his snares, was greatly downcast. He was afraid that Alexander would set the whole world in motion against him and would rouse the more important monarchs of the world for his overthrow. But since in every action of his he showed no recognition of the patience and long-suffering of God Almighty and of St. Peter like that man who did not make God his helper but relied on the greatness of his wealth, the Lord, and St. Peter too, whose Church, Frederick, casting aside all fear of God, had not shrunk from burning, grew angry with him. God cast such an epidemic of sudden death upon his army that within a week almost all the most important of his princes who were fighting with him against the Church were brought down by an untimely fate and perished miserably. We record the names of some of the more infamous among them: Frederick, Duke of Bavaria; H., Count of Nassau; Burchard, Count of Halremont; H., count of Lippe; Rainald, his Chancellor, who had been foisted upon the See of Cologne, his brother, Count Ludolf, and the Bishop of Verden, an obdurate schismatic. The other barons, the other men of arms, and the rest of the great host of warriors, as they pined away and could find no cure for their recovery, perished miserably. Their corpses lay all over the place unburied. To cut a long story short, so great a fear of an untimely death had fallen upon all that anyone who could find any way at all of getting away from the camp and of fleeing home counted himself lucky.

Then it became clear even to Frederick that he had been struck by the Hand of God. He settled with the Romans for the best terms that he could get and, not without obvious embarrassment, withdrew on 25 July. For all that, the epidemic pursued him, and as he tried to move away, he was forced to leave behind him a trail of death and mourning. The arms and the rest of the costly gear of the Germans were lost at the same time as their owners, and all their pomp was brought to naught by the vengeance of God. When Frederick with the lamentations of the dying and the groaning of the ill ringing in his ears reached Lucca and wished to pass by the public highway and Monte Bardone, he was forbidden by the Lombards from attempting to march through their territory. Demanding safe conduct from Markgrave Malaspina, he turned off, therefore, from the highway at Pontremolo, and making his way thence through deep valleys and over jagged peaks, he passed not without great loss of baggage, like a fugitive, close to Tortona, and at long last reached Pavia with few men.

But what was especially remarkable in men's eyes was that neither the memory of so many evils which he, from childhood up, had cruelly wrought, nor the fresh scourges which he had received at the hands of God and St. Peter, had softened the harshness and savagery of his heart or had turned him to doing good. On the contrary, his nature, inclined to evil from early manhood, was, it is believed, ever more bent towards it. The cities of Lombardy, therefore, which had for long experienced in their own streets his atrocities and cruelties, on seeing that his mind and intent burned against them more fiercely even than they were wont, in common deliberation declared that they ought to drive entirely from Lombardy that person who had striven to reduce the whole of Italy to shameful slavery. Accordingly they gathered a host of warriors and attacked Frederick as he marched out from Pavia. Not until they had ejected him from the whole of their territories and forced him to make his way across the Alps, did the Lombards cease from harrying the breaker and destroyer of the laws and decrees of orthodox Emperors, a man excommunicated by the Church of Rome.

In Lombardy, freed by divine assistance from tyranny and restored to its ancient liberty, a wise provision was made: it was decreed by all the Lombard cities, save only Pavia and Como, that for the future defence of all they should build a well populated city between Pavia and Asti, a city which would in future be a strong defence and a safe stronghold for the Lombards and for the Germans the greatest obstacle. And so in the year 1168 of our Lord's Incarnation, on the first day of May, of the first indiction, in the ninth year of the Pontificate of Pope Alexander, Cremona, Milan, and Piacenza, in the face of the active opposition of Pavia and the Markgrave of Monferrato, assembled their forces in equal strength near the town of Rovereto, and there designated the circuit of a city to be built for the glory of God, of St. Peter, and of the whole of Lombardy, and enclosed the site with a deep moat. All those who dwelt in the surrounding villages, with their families and all their possessions were gathered to dwell in it, namely, the inhabitants of Bosco Marengo, Foro di Gamundo, Berguglio, Oviglio, and Solero. A great and strong city was quickly built. It was their unanimous wish, for its greater glory and fame, that the city be called forever

Alessandria, out of respect for St. Peter and Pope Alexander. Alessandria lies in an attractive and very fertile district, off the main highway, protected on all sides by three rivers, and has very many good features. In the first year, its population of soldiers and warlike men of arms was said to have grown to fifteen thousand. In the following year, the consuls of the city came before Pope Alexander at Benevento to offer to him, and through him to the Holy Roman Church, the city itself as his right and possession, and of their own accord made it tributary to St. Peter. Over and above this they swore allegiance to him and his successors. They proposed that the consuls and people of Alessandria would forever renew this oath annually. When all things had been done according to custom, the consuls returned under divine guidance with the thanks, the rejoicing and the blessing of the Pope himself to their own city.

At the same time the Pontiff deposed the Bishops of Vestana and Caiazzo who had been accused and convicted of simony.

It also happened that John, the former Cardinal Priest of St. Martin, who from the beginning of this schism had not ceased, with Octavian and Guy of Crema, from persecuting the Church, fell from his horse while riding outside Viterbo, and without sign of repentance came to the end of his life by a most terrible death, for he suffered a broken neck. Guy of Crema, too, who had succeeded Octavian in the schism, was struck with an incurable disease of the foot, which left him with a limp for the rest of his life.

Since the Romans could not take their revenge on the Germans for the terrible wrong they had received, they turned at that time upon the people of Albano, who had sided with the Emperor against them, and sought to injure them. Their attacks continued against Albano until they had razed the city. For a like reason, they strove to deal in the same way with Tusculum and other stronger positions round about; but because the Church did not approve of their unjust attempts, they eventually desisted from enterprises of this sort, though unwillingly.

In the meantime, Manuel, the Emperor at Constantinople, on seeing the aforementioned Emperor Frederick in the company of schismatics vigorously attacking and persecuting the Roman Church and Pope Alexander, sent to the Pontiff at Benevento some of the more important of his secretaries with great sums of money and this message: 'Our Lord the Emperor has long had a very great desire to honour and increase the esteem for his mother the Roman Church and your person. But when he now sees Frederick, that Church's champion, whose duty it is to protect it from others and defend it, become her attacker and persecutor, his desire to serve and succour her is even stronger. And that in these days that phrase of the Gospel "and there will be one fold and one shepherd", may be fulfilled, he wishes to unite and subject his Greek Church to the Church of Rome, in that status in which we know it to have been of old, if only you are willing to restore his rights to him. For this reason he asks and begs that when the enemy of the Church has been deprived of the crown of the Roman Empire you restore it to him, as reason and justice requires. To bring this about, he is ready to bestow and expend immediately whatever you in your good pleasure consider necessary in sums of money, soldiers and armaments.' When he had heard this, the Pontiff took counsel over a long period with Bishops, Cardinals, and the more notable of the Romans, and replied in this fashion to the chief Secretary: 'We give thanks to your Lord the Emperor as to a most Christian prince and a most devoted son of St. Peter, for his devout and persevering embassies, and for the display of the good will which he bears towards the Holy Roman Church. On these accounts we listen with pleasure to his most affectionate words. In so far as we can, in obedience to God, we wish with fatherly kindness to fulfil his requests. But what he asks goes very deep and is exceedingly complicated, and since the decrees of the holy Fathers forbid such requests on account of their inherent difficulties, we neither can nor ought to grant our assent under terms of this sort, since by reason of the office entrusted to us by God it is fitting that we be the authors and guardians of the peace.' Thus therefore, taking back from the hands of the pontiff the gifts he had brought, the Secretary returned to his master with all the money. The two Cardinals whom the same Pontiff had appointed as ambassadors to the same Emperor followed close after.

At this time Guy of Crema, who even while he continued to dwell in the Church of St. Peter persisted in the error of which he had been the author, was inflicted by that same apostle with a cancer of the kidneys and breathlessness in the lungs. A fetid pus flowed from his body until, still impenitent, he breathed his unhappy last and fell prey to a most foul death. This death inspired some rhymer's verses, thus:

F

The godless pride of Octavian and mad Guy has crumbled,
And their unseasonable power.
But through reason and faith Alexander soars high, a second Peter;
He stands, now firm on the rock, hereafter set in the heavens.

Their two chief members having been taken away out of the midst of their abomination of desolation, the remaining crowd of schismatics was cast down to the depth of despair, since there was no member of their Church remaining whom they could put at her head. They chose therefore a certain John, a former Abbot of Strumi, an apostate, a slippery fellow, gluttonous and giddy, and set him as the third horned beast upon the seat of pestilence, though not without the laughter and derision of many. Like obstinate infidels they worshipped the abomination and presumed with devilish instinct to give him veneration. This apostate joined the depraved and vicious of whom he was to remain the chief for so long, because he was deservedly despised and hated by all good men. His supporters and the intimates of his household were nothing more than apostates, pimps, buffoons, fugitives from monasteries and convicted criminals, thieves and footpads who bestowed upon this destitute and poverty-stricken person what they had stolen from travellers and pilgrims.

In the meantime the Emperor Frederick, perceiving that the two idols which he had set up had been cast down by the judgement of God, and that the third, too, had been chosen and elevated not from the body of the Church, but from the mob of his accomplices, was inwardly deeply grieved, since his cause had come to nothing and that of Pope Alexander was ever growing stronger and achieving greater things. But that he might not seem to be overthrown in his evil proposal and entirely brought to naught, like the clever and most astute man that he was, he pretended to venerate the Beast, and ordered his supporters to maintain him and show him their favour. But after a short space of time he returned to his customary cunning and in order to acquire the support of all, simulated a display of good will and a pious desire for the reform of the Church and the peace of the Empire. To such an extent did he lower himself in his cunning that he sent the Bishop of Bamberg, who was ever a good Catholic at heart, to come before Pope Alexander at Benevento. He gave power to the Bishop to make concord and peace between himself and the Pope in accordance with the credentials with which he had furnished him. He enjoined him also to reveal these matters to the Pontiff alone. Indeed, as was afterwards clear, it is recognized that he acted in this fashion to drive by this piece of trickery a wedge between the Church and the Lombards and so separate the one from the others. The Pontiff, on being informed of the arrival of the Bishop and on learning that nothing had been entrusted to him in the matter of the Lombards, had no hesitation in divining the wiliness and toils of the sender, and so took the advice of his Bishops and Cardinals. He sent in haste letters and messengers to the Lombards, gave reassurance to their doubting and wavering minds, and informed them that it was his advice that they send to his court from each of their towns one discreet and suitable person who could speak for the whole community. With these envoys he wished to negotiate concerning the message of peace and union borne by the Bishop and make whatever dispositions and ordinances would have to be made as a result. So certain trustworthy and experienced men were elected by the community of the Lombards and appointed to attend on the Pontiff.

The Bishop, on his arrival in Campagna, announced to the Pontiff, that, since he had been forbidden to enter the lands of the King of Sicily, the Pope should deign to return to the Patrimony of St. Peter in Campagna that they might confer there. The Pontiff therefore was pleased to grant his request and returned from Benevento with his brother Bishops and the envoys of the Lombards to Campagna to await the Bishop in the city of Veroli. On the next day when the Pope according to custom had taken his seat in full consistory Eberhard of Bamberg arrived. He entered with respect into the presence of Pope Alexander, did him reverence and said: 'My Lord, the Emperor Frederick has sent me to you, and has strictly enjoined me that I speak to you alone, and to you alone reveal the messages he has entrusted to me.' Again and again the Pope answered him: 'It is quite useless for you to explain to me alone those matters to which I ought not to give a reply without the knowledge and agreement of my brothers and of the Lombards.' He could, therefore, only with difficulty obtain agreement that he alone should hear him first, and that he should afterwards communicate with he had heard to those whom he wished. But finally the Pope gave him attentive hearing in private as he had requested. The Bishop, first revealed many and varied matters, then asserted firmly that the Emperor wished to take no further action against his person and would consider valid all his ordinances and order them to be observed

79

by other men. But he spoke in such a veiled and ambiguous manner about the Papacy and the obedience that was due to it that one could not take from them at all a Catholic sense. When the Pope pressed him vigorously again and again to speak on these matters not in parables but in plain truth he confessed that since he had been strictly forbidden to do so, he dared neither to explain them nor to alter them. When he had heard the Emperor's envoy out, the Pontiff, since he could elicit no more information from the Bishop, withdrew to the more private chamber where he had sent the brethren with the Lombards, and related to one and all what he had heard.

Beloved brother in Christ, since you have brought, as if you were unaware of the circumstances, a message of this kind to us, who are not ignorant of the clever tricks and wiles of him who sent it, you make us wonder at your good sense. For since, as you declare, the Emperor is willing, God be thanked, to accept the ordinances made by us, and to have them validated by other men, yet is not prepared to consent to our person, who, though unworthy, has succeeded canonically to St. Peter in the Apostolic See, what does there remain to be done, except to give glory and worship to God, and on our part to renounce the Emperor? The entire Church of God, the other Christian Kings and Princes have already adjudged our cause canonical and everywhere obey us. If therefore he wishes to be numbered among the sheep which God entrusted to St. Peter to be pastured by him, why does he still desist from bowing his head to the same Prince of the Apostles and to unite himself to the one Catholic Church? But for him, we should be ready and willing to give him honour and respect before the other Princes of the world, and preserve for him his rights in their entirety, if only he would respect with filial devotion his mother the Holy Roman Church who carried him to the highest place in the Empire, and preserve her freedom.

After this, rebuked and advised in a brotherly spirit, Eberhard of Bamberg, conducted by the Lombards, returned to Frederick.

Since the Pontiff was residing at the city of Veroli, and the Romans were pressing their attacks against Tusculum more vigorously than was their wont, their Lord, Raino, stricken with a great fear, contrary to the allegiance which he had given to the Pontiff, foolishly and imprudently gave the town in exchange to Giovanni Maledetto, who had been appointed City Prefect by Frederick. He also absolved the people of Tusculum from the fealty that bound them to him. And so, when he had given this town into the hands and power of Giovanni, he received from him Montefiascone and Borgo San Flaviano with their dependencies, which, all know, belong to the Patrimony of St. Peter. Upon this, Pope Alexander, when he saw the Patrimony of St. Peter so insolently divided and given away, could not but be indignant and seriously perturbed at both men, since half of Tusculum with Montefiascone and Borgo San Flaviano by right of ownership belonged to the Church of Rome alone. On the other hand, since the Romans held both in great hatred, to gain possession they attacked Tusculum all the more strongly with ceaseless assaults. At this, Giovanni Maledetto grew extremely terrified, abandoned the town and fled. At the same time Raino perceived that he had been tricked and, spurned and driven out by the soldiers and people of Montefiascone, abandoned that territory too, and, full of shame, tried to return to Tusculum whose inhabitants he had so indiscreetly released from their allegiance. But because he had released them from his overlordship and their allegiance and rashly subjected them to another, they not only refused to receive him, but also drove him from all parts of their territory. Deprived of every counsel and assistance he fled to his mother, the Church of Rome which he had so rashly injured, and, like the prodigal son, asked for pardon and mercy from his lord, Pope Alexander, and his brother Bishops, placing himself and whatever rights he appeared to have in the town of Tusculum at the Pontiff's good pleasure and mercy. But the people of Tusculum had forestalled Raino and had, of their own accord, surrendered themselves and their city and all that was in it to the lordship of St. Peter and the power of the Pontiff. Thus it came about that Raino himself made a gift of the town by means of letters patent, to the Pope and his successors. The text of the letters follows:

In the name of the Lord. In the year of the Incarnation of our Lord 1170, the third indiction, in the eleventh year of the pontificate of the Lord Alexander III, on this day, the eighth day of the month of August, I, Raino, son of Tolomeo, formerly of Tusculum, with no man objecting to or forbidding or bringing force to bear against me, being of sound mind, freely and voluntarily, in the presence of the undersigned, H. Cardinal Bishop of Ostia; Bernard, Cardinal Bishop of Porto; the Cardinal Priests Hu. of Santa Croce; I. of SS. John and Paul; V of St. Peter-and-Vincula; Al. of San Lorenzo in Lucina; B. of Santa Pudenziana; P. of San Lorenzo in Damaso; I. of San Marco and T. of San Vitale; and of the Cardinal Deacons I. of Santa Maria in Cosmidin; A.

of San Teodoro; C. of Sant' Adriano; H. of Sant' Eustachio; V. of Santi Sergio e Baccho and P. of Santa Maria in Aciro, unconditionally and relying only on your mercy, do give, surrender, grant, renounce, and entrust to you, my lord, Pope Alexander, and through you to your Catholic successors and to the holy Roman Church, the town of Tusculum with its citadel, houses, domains, squares, banners, courts, and all its customs and appurtenances, as are found on a site not far from the City, and are contained within its boundaries, with ploughland and waste, vineyards, gardens, woods, chestnut groves, meadows, pastures, springs and watercourses, mills, and whatever or in whatever way in the same town and its citadel or territory by right of inheritance, whether by tenement or fee or any title whatsoever I or my predecessors have held, possessed, had or appeared to have, at any time of your predecessors or of you or of the aforesaid holy Roman Church. And from this hour henceforth you may have the power of entering upon it, of holding, possessing, disposing of, working, enjoying, arbitrating, enfeoffing, and doing to it whatever it may please you and your successors and the holy Roman Church to do, in perpetuity. And I both for my own part and for the part of my heirs promise you and your successors to defend all these presents at the bar of justice, should there be need. But if I do not do this, or be unwilling or unable, or, which God forbid, any of my successors or anyone else, we shall pay to you a fine of a hundred gold pounds, and the fine having been paid, this charter will be confirmed. This I have asked Achille, the secretary of the holy Roman Church, to write in the month and indiction named above.

This is the sign of the hand of Raino at whose request this charter was made. Giovanni di Supino, witness. Pietro di Babuco, witness. Pietro the Butler, witness. Mattafellone, nephew of the Lord Pope, witness. Galiota, witness. Alberto, the doorkeeper, witness.

I, Achille, secretary of the holy Roman Church, have completed and finished my task.

When these things had been done in this way, Pope Alexander sent his subdeacon Pietro di Gaeta and the nobleman Giovanni di Supino to Tusculum, to take possession in their turn of the town and the citadel overlooking it, as the property and domain of the Apostolic See. This was done without delay and brought to completion in the correct fashion. But Alexander himself left Veroli and went on to Tusculum only when he had celebrated the Nativity of the Blessed Virgin Mary. On the Vigil of St. Luke he entered the town itself in pomp and ceremony, and during twenty-six months resided in the palace of the citadel as its Lord.

But the people of Rome, who were intent on destroying this town, were roused to great indignation against the Pontiff over this matter and were very disturbed. They asserted with an appearance of superiority that he ought not to accept or protect that town at whose hands the Roman people themselves had recently suffered such a serious misfortune. They threatened with loud cries that unless he abandoned that place entirely they would strive with all their strength to bring upon him whatever ill or opposition they could. Although the Pontiff answered them with all gentleness and patience, and carefully explained the clear right which the Apostolic See had long had to that town, promising that the City of Rome would obtain a continuing benefit from a place which had come into the hands of the Church, and that no further evil would arise from it, yet there was no way for him to placate the Roman populace and draw them back from their wickedness. Indeed the people themselves have become quite unlike their forefathers in the days of St. Paul, and daily fall lower. For down the centuries nothing has been so well known as Roman wantonness. They are factious in their dealings with one another and jealous of their neighbours; they know neither how to be ruled nor how to rule; to their superiors they are disloyal, and to their subjects unbearable; they have taught their mouths to utter noble words while performing petty deeds. But let us return to our subject.

Since the Roman populace had risen against the people of Tusculum with neither reason nor just cause, and spared neither their persons nor their possessions, but laid waste in a spirit of enmity their vines and crops, the Pontiff reluctantly allowed his household to fight force with force, and to oppose his adversaries to their distress. Then certain men-at-arms from Tusculum with certain foot-soldiers went up to where the roads issued from the City and to the grazing-grounds of the beasts of burden, and boldly captured right to the gates of the City whatever men or beasts they found and carried off to their own parts a large number of living creatures without loss to themselves. Acting in this fashion by day and by night they restrained the impertinence of the Romans so severely, that no-one could travel with calm mind between Rome and Tusculum in security, nor was anyone able to go out safely to his ploughing or sowing. But after many losses had been inflicted by one side and the other and after holding various conferences, at length each side agreed of their own accord, that the Pontiff, like the loving father of all, for the honour of the City of Rome and for the sake

83

of peace, would allow the walls of Tusculum, save only those of the citadel, to be lowered to an agreed height. In return, the Roman people firmly pledged to forgive entirely and pardon all the injuries which the people of Tusculum had inflicted on them, and to make a true and lasting peace. Over and above, to remove all doubt entirely from the minds of all, the people of Rome promised to confirm the peace with as many oaths of Roman citizens as pleased the Pontiff and the people of Tusculum. So eight hundred men, chosen by name from among that people, at the request of the Pontiff, and at the good pleasure of Tusculum, took their oaths on the holy Gospels as had been promised, and as each took his oath it was taken again in the hearts of the people, who acclaimed them.

When the oaths had been taken and the other agreements arranged according to usage on either side, and when the outer ramparts were already levelled, and the turrets which had been erected on the outer walls were already lying in ruins, and when the strength of the walls themselves had been shaken and broken, the people, forgetful of their oaths, were not content to observe the measures fixed beforehand as had been agreed, but against the troth they had given and the oaths that had been taken, against, moreover, the prohibition of Pope Alexander and his brother Bishops, they shamelessly pulled down all the walls of Tusculum and those of its citadel. What is there now that we can say in truth of the Roman people, except that their sins, their faithlessness, and fickleness must be broadcast to the whole world, Yet, though the Romans were vicious and barbarous and brooked no rule, they were the particular charge of the Roman Pontiff, and therefore he could not but make quite clear that he would not in his fatherly kindness allow their backsliding and that he was eager to recall them to the path of goodness as far as lay in his power. In truth, it is care that is demanded of the Roman Pontiff, not cure, for the Gospel says: 'Have a care for him', and not 'Cure or heal him'. Indeed, 'The doctor has not always the power to discover the sick man'. The Apostle also says: 'I have toiled more than anyone else.' He did not say: 'I was more successful than anyone else, or I gained a greater profit than anyone else.' On the contrary, the man who has been taught by God has learnt that he will receive according to his toil, not according to his gain. Because of this the blessed Pontiff Alexander, making light of the injuries he had suffered, strove with all his might to convert straightway to the path of righteousness and well-doing that people whose charge

84

had been laid upon him by our Lord, and whose wrongdoing and sins he must, as Christ's vicar, bear.

At the same time the very sad news of the murder of the Archbishop of Canterbury, St. Thomas, and the charges against the King of the English came to the ears of the Apostolic See. As his notoriety grew, the King not undeservedly feared that the Roman Church would exact dire penalty against his person for so great a crime, unless it were to have clear understanding of his innocence. He sent accordingly to the Supreme Pontiff prudent men of the Church, giving them authority to swear upon his soul to pay heed to the Pope's instructions in the matter of this murder which had brought him into ill-repute. The envoys coming to Tusculum on the Thursday of Holy Week before Easter, when the Pontiff was on the point of going to church, presented themselves before the Apostolic presence, and explaining what had been imposed upon them by the same King, offered to take the oath we have described. Then the Pontiff, having held a council of his brother Bishops, came out in Consistory and in the hearing of all, received the oath, as it had been worded and phrased by the Cardinals, from the envoys and granted a truce to the King. Subsequently the Pontiff sent two of his brother-Bishops, Albert, Cardinal Priest of San Lorenzo in Lucina and Theodwin, Cardinal Priest of Vestina, to France so that the guilt or innocence of the King might become clear to them at the place at which so detestable a deed had been committed.

The King, learning of the envoys of the Apostolic See, put aside all those urgent affairs which he was then negotiating in Ireland and returned in haste to Normandy and at Caen came before the envoys humbly and reverently with his Bishops and barons for a second time, ready to abide by their command, as had previously been promised through his envoys. However, since nobody appeared to impeach him with the crime imputed to him, the King made atonement in his own person for his acts in this manner before the envoys and a great crowd of Bishops and barons and others both clerical and lay:

I, Henry, King, swear upon these holy Gospels that I neither plotted nor knew of nor commanded to be executed the death of the saintly Thomas; and when I learnt that the crime had been committed, I was as grief-stricken and sorrowful as if I had learnt that my own son had been slain. But in this matter I cannot hold myself excused because the holy man would not have been done to death had it not been for my troubled state and the anger which I had conceived against him. On account of this, since I seem to have given cause for his death, I shall send, without delay, to Jerusalem at my expense for the defence of Christendom, two hundred soldiers, and these are to be stationed there throughout a whole year, or I shall at least pay for the same number as much as it costs to keep them there for a year. I shall also take the sign of the Cross of Our Lord for a space of three years and shall set out thither in my own person, unless by the permission of the Roman Pontiff I may remain here. Those unlawful customs which in my time I have introduced throughout the length and breadth of my kingdom I also entirely abrogate and forbid to be observed. Moreover I shall allow appeals to the Apostolic See to be made freely, and I shall prevent nobody in this matter. Besides all these, I and my elder son the King, swear that both we and our successors shall have and hold the Kingdom of England from the Lord Pope Alexander and his Catholic successors and that we and our successors shall not consider ourselves for ever as the true Kings of England until they themselves hold us as Catholic Kings.

While these things were being done in France, the Romans holding fast to their foolishness would not allow the Shepherd and Bishop of their souls to enter the City with his brother Bishops and the Cardinals, though they desired to do so; nor carry out in their churches their due offices. Since they despised the word of God which they had been the first to hear, the Pope left Tusculum with his brother Bishops and went off to the Patrimony of Blessed Peter in Campagna, there to dwell until the Lord should give better times to His Church.

In the meantime, since the glory of the English Blessed Thomas shone everywhere by God's good pleasure in a blaze of miracles, and not only his friends, but even his persecutors besought the pardon of their sins, and without cease drew near to his tomb to demand the blessings of salvation, the Roman Pontiff, at the request of his clergy and the peoples of France, canonized the martyr by his Apostolic authority, and ordered him inscribed in the roll of the saints. On the day of the Purification of Blessed Mary, he summoned the Bishops and Abbots of Campagna and at Segni celebrated the rites of the Mass with special solemnity and ordered the day of his martyrdom, 29 December, to be kept for ever as his festival day. For this reason the Church in the West was filled with great joy and the name of the glorious martyr was daily enhanced by the display of his powers, so that even among people not English his honour steadily grew greater. Through his merits Almighty God in the sight of men raised the dead, gave sight to the blind, hearing to the deaf, and the power of walking to the lame, cleansed lepers, cured the sick, freed the possessed, and willed to work many other miracles besides through him. And so very many of the faithful raised churches in his honour for the praise and glory of our Creator and enriched them with goods and estates.

Two years and three months having passed since the death of the martyr, the elder son of the King of England, whom the latter had himself, out of fatherly affection, raised to kingly power, rose against his father in a most criminal way but not, it is believed, without a judgement of divine retribution. Together with his mother and brothers he rashly attempted to drive him right out of his kingdom which thus was divided between two parties. Of the barons of Aquitaine some stood in arms with the son, and others with the father. In order to accomplish so detestable an overthrow, the King of the French took the younger King, to whom he had given his daughter to wife, into his protection, and strove with all his might to assist and maintain him against his father. For these reasons there was a growth of great evil, and, their sins seeking requital, the son sought the destruction of his father, and the father thirsted for the blood of his son. Finally large armies were got ready on both sides and the younger King with his father-in-law, the King of the French, invaded Normandy to fight against his father. On the other side the elder King of the English strove with all his might to defend his land and in every way to combat force with force. Without delay warriors rose to arms everywhere, looted, put towns to flames, stormed castles, violated churches and did not desist from other acts of impiety done cruelly throughout the whole of Aquitaine. And as these evils daily increased their lord Pope Alexander, conscious of the obligations of his office, wanted to provide protection against the devastation and damage. He sent to those regions P., Cardinal Priest of St. Chrysogonus. He ordered him to take as his companions the Bishops and other clerics of both parties into his confidence and diligently to take upon himself the task of discovering how the Kings themselves could be called back to peace and concord. Accordingly, as the legate arrived at the right moment, the prelates succeeded in making the prelates of the churches and the other clerics as well as prudent men intervene between the two parties with such great ardour that they, with the assistance of the Lord, recalled each to the benefits of unity and peace.

At the same time, in the fifteenth year of the pontificate of Pope Alexander, the Emperor Frederick, invaded Lombardy for the fifth time at the request of the citizens of Pavia and the Markgrave of Monferrato. He came by Mont Cenis, and descending to the plain with a great company encamped near Susa on 29 September. On the next day, unable to conceal further the rage that burned within him, he set fire to the town. This was the first of his hateful crimes. Afterwards he turned his army towards Asti to carry out the rest of his evil intentions. For he had about him a great army of barbarian people, men accustomed to the practice of war, men most evil, rapacious desperadoes whom he had gathered together from Flanders and the regions that lie thereabout, and whom, since they have love for no man, none loves. The Lombards, one in heart and will, because they had had intelligence of Frederick's return while he was as yet at a distance, had fortified their towns and citadels well before his arrival and, like warlike and strong men, stood dauntless to resist him. To aid the citizens of Asti therefore, with whom they had long been in alliance, they sent sturdy men, farsighted in counsel and tried in the exercise of arms, to restore their spirits in the face of the enemy's onslaught that was coming upon them and to urge them to fight, when the occasion demanded, for the maintenance of their liberty. But Asti, foreseeing for itself a worse fate at a later date, unwisely withdrew from its alliance with the Lombards. They fell on their faces before Frederick and surrendered their town into his possession and power.

After the submission of Asti, Frederick in his overweening pride attempted to proceed swiftly to the destruction of Alessandria with the men and the Markgrave of Monferrato. This was the town the Lombards had recently built in honour of St. Peter. But since in every one of his actions he was in opposition to God and to His Church, Almighty God in a wonderful way stood in the path of his evil plan and upset it. So great a downpour of rain did He send on a sudden from heaven, that every river overflowed its banks and every plain became a marsh. When the people of Alessandria saw the assistance that had been granted to them from Heaven, they who had already prepared for flight from fear of the terrible monarch found their strength and spirit again and, putting their trust in the intercession of the holy Apostles Peter and Paul and casting aside all fear, prepared themselves manfully to withstand the vast host of their enemies. But although the bitterness of the winter and

88

the threatening difficulty of rain and snow urged Frederick not to advance on Alessandria, he nevertheless went forth in his strength and somehow fortified his camp which was pitched hard by the town in its sodden fields. And so, looking about and seeing that apart from a ditch and the nearby river Tanaro the town did not enjoy the protection of either walls or towers, he underestimated the town and foolishly expected that at the first assault he would utterly destroy it. Gathering together every strength of his army, he made a most heavy assault upon Alessandria. He brought engines of various kinds up to the mounds and long carried on a ferocious struggle with them in an atrocious manner. But with the aid of the Lord the people of Alessandria prevailed. They captured their enemies' engines by assault and not without loss forced the whole barbarian throng to flee to their tents with heavy damage. When he saw himself overpowered, Frederick was inflamed with even greater anger, and so, against the advice and wish of his Princes, he made ready to linger in siege operations until he obtained his victory. But since the bitterness of winter was drawing near, and the army was suffering from a lack of all necessary supplies, his great herd of horses began to waste away entirely, and the soldiers' gear began to be squandered for little gain. And yet neither on account of these nor other hardships did the Emperor's anger desist from the assault upon Alessandria, though the city's resistance grew ever more bitter. Eventually, when he could neither by threats nor blandishments nor promises in any way persuade the citizens to surrender, he secretly had tunnels made by which he hoped to enter and break into the town unexpectedly. But since the Lord opposed him, he deserved to incur grievous loss just when he believed victory and triumph to be within reach.

And now, when the town had been closely besieged for four months and was suffering lack in many things, it asked for the strength and assistance of the Lombard League. Then did an immense League of the towns of Lombardy quickly assemble and by common consent decree that it should straightway hasten in strong company to Alessandria with a great quantity of victuals and other necessaries. In the middle of Lent all the townsfolk and nobles of Liguria, the March, and Emilia assembled at Piacenza, and when all things required for war had been correctly ordered and ordained, with boats and wagons laden with food and weapons, they left the town. They advanced with a great force of soldiers and footsoldiers, of military engines and money chests towards Alessandria, and on Palm Sunday pitched camp hard by Tortona, no further than ten miles from the camp of Frederick.

But when the Germans and Lombards gazed upon one another, fear and dullness entered Frederick's mind, as he saw that a frightening mass of armed men stood against him, drawn up in battle order. Hence, turning to the accustomed wiles of his cleverness, he addressed, mildly and deceitfully, the following words to the people of Alessandria: 'Tomorrow is Good Friday, when every Christian man offers most devoutly his worship, and therefore out of reverence for the Crucified I grant and bestow upon you out of my imperial graciousness a truce and safety until the Monday.' When some of the people, having accepted this assurance and suspecting no evil, were sleeping peacefully in their houses, their deceiver ordered, about the first watch of the night, the more courageous of his men-at-arms to enter the city through the subterranean tunnels, while he himself stood in armour at the gates with his whole army, waiting for those whom he had sent on ahead to enter the town, so that he could hear the sounds of their shouts. He planned, while the battle was growing every moment more fierce within, to make a violent onslaught from without through the gates and seize the town. But the city was set free in a moment from such a wicked betrayal and the evil that had been devised was turned back upon the heads of the wicked by the Lord and this seemed wonderful in the eyes of all. For there is nothing more just than that those who devise death should perish by their own device. For the truth itself which speaks of such miscreants in this fashion cannot lie: 'Their grief will be turned upon their own heads, and their iniquity will descend upon them', and again: 'He who prepares a pit for his neighbour falleth into it himself.' When then the watchmen who were guarding the city saw that whole bodies of men-at-arms had entered it, they cried out loudly for the people to rise quickly to arms and drive out the invaders. The citizens, immediately aroused, swiftly seized their arms, and like lions fell bodily upon their enemies. With the aid of St. Peter whom they saw at their head mounted on a white charger and clad in flashing armour, they brought their enemies to the ground, and then, at the point of their swords compelled all who had escaped death to go up to the mounds, from which they were cast down. All those besides who had not yet come up from the tunnels to the upper air was suffocated by falling soil. The people opened the gates and went out with courage at the high and fell upon the army of the faithless Frederick with their swords, keeping it up until the dawn of the Saturday, so that the whole place, as far as his camp, was stained with the blood of the dead. Moreover, the wooden fort also which Frederick had carefully manned for the ruin of the town with the pick of his brave soldiers, was attacked so long and vigorously that it burnt down together with its defenders.

Frederick, when he saw that Divine Majesty was against him, feared that he would incur destruction at the hands of the army of the Lombards that was advancing against him. He was therefore forced, with shame, to abandon the siege. During the following night he had the camp burnt down and in the dawn of Easter Sunday he made his way with all his men towards Pavia. But since he could not avoid cutting across the Lombard army's lines he wanted to encamp near the Lombards in the village which is known as Santa Giulietta. He did not fear that he would be attacked by them, unless he himself provoked them to battle. The Lombards had not yet discovered what Almighty God had on the previous day wrought with the aid of Alessandria. When they saw Frederick coming against them with flying standards, they took up arms and manfully stood there in armour before him, prepared to do battle. But at first they were watching what he would decide to do, whether he would start to fight (which seemed unlikely because he had much fewer men than they had) or whether he would set up camp peacefully and harm nobody. He himself on that day, which the Lord had made peaceful, made his camp in the village. When dawn broke on the Monday, certain of the nobility, whom neither of the parties held in any suspicion, went in humble fashion to Frederick first, and then to the Lombards with this address: 'What greater foolishness or what more remarkable evil can be thought of or practised than that a Lord should attempt to deprive his servant of all which is his by right and take possession of it by violent means, unless it is that servants should do the same to their lord. Let each side be content with what is rightfully its own, and lest such great evils do not come to an end, let the peace between both of you that you so long for again return with the help of the Lord.' Then the Emperor, after many entreaties had been made now from one side and now from the other, sighed and made answer in this way: 'Saving the rights of the Empire, I am ready in this dispute to submit to the arbitration of good men chosen from each side.' Later the assembly of the

Lombards said: 'Saving the freedom of the Church of Rome and of ourselves for which we are fighting, we do the same.' Straightway there were chosen by Frederick, Philip, Archbishop elect of Cologne, Walfred of Pozasca, a noble of Turin, and Rainerio di San Nazario of Pavia. The Lombards chose Gerardo Pisto of Milan, Alberto di Gambera of Brescia, and C. of Verona. Each side cheerfully reached a compromise through them. Afterwards the Lombards went reverently to Frederick and did him honour, and they were kindly received and honoured by him.

When these things had been done on both sides, Frederick allowed the army to depart, and with his wife, sons and household went down to the town of Pavia. The Lombards, glad to return to their own towns, met the men of Cremona with their chariots and their expeditionary force. For the latter, because of their respect for their friendship with the men of Pavia, were always wavering in the performance of their duty as members of the League of the towns. They had so delayed their decision to go out with the others that the expedition of the League was put to considerable trouble on account of that delay. When Cremona learnt that the peace had been made without her she was abashed in her shame. Then the people of Cremona waxed exceedingly wroth against their consuls and repaid in a harsh manner the insult given to their town. They razed the foundations of the consuls' palaces and houses, seized all their possessions, and appointed other consuls to serve for the rest of the term of those who had been deposed.

Although the Lombard towns had made treaties of mutual peace and harmony with Frederick, they knew his craftiness and so took particular care for the future. For this reason they took special care to renew the oaths of the alliance, and in all matters showed a greater caution.

When Frederick had been staying at Pavia a rather long time, and saw that all his schemes were turning out badly, in order to win the favour of the clerics and the common people he was eager to restore again peace to the Roman Church and declared publicly that he wanted to put this plan before anything else. Therefore he sent letters and members of his household to the Bishops of Ostia and Porto and to the Cardinal of St. Peter-ad-Vincula, bidding them to come to him in safety to restore the peace between the Church and the Empire, so that face to face they might be able to deal with one another and gain, by the help of the Lord, the longed-for goal with honour to the Church. When this message came to the notice of the Apostolic See, it was not undeservedly treated by all with suspicion, for if past experience was an indication, one could be certain as to what would happen in the future, and also because at no time had Frederick ever seemed, in any way, inclined towards good works. But since, as St. Augustine says, what is uncertain ought always to be seen in the best possible light, and because peace is described as something that is not only to be desired but also to be pursued, Pope Alexander, on the advice of all his brothers sent the persons we have mentioned with full instructions to the presence of the Prince with all due ceremony. As the envoys went their separate ways through various regions, the people rejoiced in the Lord at the happy sight and when they beheld their credentials, they presented to them a large number of children to be blessed. The Bishop of Porto and the Cardinal of St. Peter-ad-Vincula journeyed through Spoleto, Imola and Bologna. They reached Piacenza and there awaited for some days the arrival of the Bishop of Ostia who with pomp and ceremony had travelled through Pisa and Lucca. From Lucca, after conferring with the rulers of the towns of Lombardy about the terms which had been imposed upon them, they went on to Lodi. When their conference had come to an end, they heard that the Bishop of Porto Romano had arrived at Piacenza and hastened there to meet him.

When the three legates of the Apostolic See were reunited, they announced their arrival to Frederick, asking him to signify immediately to them what he wanted them to do. He answered kindly, bidding them to cross the Po and come to him in safety. Then the envoys left Piacenza with a great assembly of clerics and soldiers, went in procession to the bank of the Po and, crossing in boats which had been made ready, entered Pavia, where they were welcomed and treated kindly. On the following day, with the Emperor seated in public among his Princes and a great gathering of peoples, the legates approached his presence together. When they had entered his presence and were seated close to him and were facing him on their faldstools, the Emperor, doffing the cap which he was wearing, greeted the envoys in German, while an interpreter translated his remarks. He stated that their arrival was a source of great pleasure to him and that he held their persons in great esteem and with smiling countenance he urged them to lay before him the proposals of which they were the bearers.

Then the Bishop of Ostia arose in their midst and when all were

93

G

listening to him, with joyful countenance, made the following reply:

Your greeting, Lord Emperor, is pleasing and very acceptable to us, the greeting of a most distinguished Prince and of a most outstanding ruler. But the greetings you have addressed to us are very provocative because in the present instance we are unable to give you our greeting in turn as we wish, on account of the strictures that your sin lays upon us. May Almighty God through the unlimited clemency of His bounty give concord and the peace of unity between His most holy Spouse the Church and your Empire, so that what we cannot now do without a scruple of conscience, we may be able to perform in the very near future through the mercy of God. We have come in particular at your summons to carry out as far as lies in our power this work of piety. Presuming not on our own powers or on our own merits, we put the completion of this task in His trust Who said when He sent out his disciples to preach: 'I have chosen you and appointed you that you may go and bring forth fruit, and that your fruit may remain. . . .'

And starting with the beginning of the schism he spoke so feelingly of all the injuries done to the Church and the manifest harm to the Empire, and spoke so boldly for harmony and peace on each side that all his audience marvelled and with joy in their hearts said to one another; 'It is not this man who is speaking, but the Spirit of God the Father, Who dwells in him.' Then in a few words he reproved the Emperor, rebuking him soundly for his hardness of heart, for when those four persons who had gone over to him from the Body of the Church had been carried off by the judgement of God, and when everyone had accepted a single Roman Pontiff as the father and shepherd of their souls, he ought not further to have been an enemy of Catholic unity, but to have believed in the One, Holy and Apostolic Church and been humbly obedient to her. After this, the Bishop of Porto and the Cardinal of St. Peter-ad-Vincula spoke briefly on the same subjects, and sought, now by kind words, now by harsh ones, to turn the mind of the Emperor towards the benefits of peace. Then the Emperor, greatly smitten in his conscience, gave a mild reply, and promised his complete assent to the longed-for peace. He displayed the grief of his heart with which he declared he had inwardly burned ever since the Church of God had been driven hither and thither by the scourge of so great a tribulation. When the speeches had been completed all returned at the same time to their lodgings.

But after a short space of time, the envoys came together again at Frederick's court. They discussed for very many days, now with the Emperor alone, now with him and his counsellors, how the benefits of peace might be given to Frederick and to the Church of Rome and her allies, the Lombards, the King of Sicily, and the Emperor in Constantinople. In order to give the best possible chance to these negotiations with the Lombards it was decided that they should take place in the absence of the Emperor. The Emperor, therefore, gave authority to negotiate to his Chancellor, Christian, to Philip the Archbishop-elect of Cologne, and to Arduin, his Protonotary, so that they could discuss the disputed clauses and obtain whatever compromise they could and refer everything to his attention. They therefore held very frequent negotiations about the peace to be made with the rulers of Lombardy and the envoys, now in the towns, now in the outskirts, just as seemed most convenient to them. But when the demands of either side were referred to the Emperor for his attention, in all matters he went beyond the bounds of moderation: from the Church he demanded in spiritual matters what can nowhere be discovered ever to have been granted to a layman; and from the Lombards, more than that with which the Emperors Charles, Louis, and Otto had been content. Since Frederick was on no account willing to withdraw his wicked demands, and since the envoys were reluctant to deviate from the rules and statutes of the holy Fathers, they left him in the toils of his error and returned under the guidance of the Lord to the Papal presence and the college of their brethren. The Lombards for their part manfully defended the ancient possession of their liberty and withstood Frederick's wickedness even more bravely than was their wont. By means of frequent invasions they also subdued Pavia and with them, the Markgraves and Como.

It was now that Pope Alexander at the request of the Archbishop of Milan, and of the Bishops of the Province, and of the Rectors of the Lombard towns raised the Church of Alessandria to the status of a bishopric. He secured the election of Arduin, a subdeacon of the Roman Church, who was consecrated by the Metropolitan of Milan as his suffragan.

Furthermore he deprived the Bishop of Pavia of the privilege of the crozier and pallium of an Archbishop, since that city had gone over to the heresiarch Octavian and the Emperor despite their excommunication and had dared, although the city had given satisfaction for their crime, to recall Frederick to Italy to the great danger of the Church and of the Lombards. For this city, as the Annals of the Roman Pontiffs declare, was of old a refuge for Kings who persecuted the Church and the Bishops of Rome. For example Aistulf, King of the Lombards, seized the Exarchate of Ravenna with violence from Pope Stephen II, and in the manner of a wicked and abandoned fellow who had put behind him all fear of God and St. Peter, brought other grave ills upon the Church of Rome and the City. This was the reason why the King of the Franks, Pepin of venerated memory, at the request of the same Pope had entered Lombardy for a second time with a great army, and shut up the rebellious Aistulf in Pavia until he had fulfilled the instructions and good pleasure of the Pope and restored to the Church all he had taken from her. Aistulf's successor in the monarchy, Desiderius, in spite of this, persecuted Pope Hadrian I and his Church and City impiously and with great cruelty. Again, it was for this reason that Charlemagne at the request of the Pope himself laid so close a siege for six months to Pavia, the city in which Desiderius had shut himself up, that he seized the King and his Queen, and took him back in chains to the Kingdom of the Franks. It is therefore no surprise that in these present times, this faithless city has received schismatics and excommunicates to spite the unity of the Church, and that she toils with all her strength to support them.

In the year of our Lord's Incarnation 1176, the seventeenth year of the pontificate of Pope Alexander, about the end of June, while Frederick was waiting at the place he had appointed for it the army he had summoned from Germany, he took counsel with Pavia. With a few men he went incognito to Como, joined his army, placed under his colours the whole population of that town and made a sudden invasion of the territory of Milan. He began to sack and ravage the towns and fields. For he had arranged with Pavia that when he invaded the territories of Milan, he would give the signal which they had agreed on beforehand, and her townsfolk would come in force to his assistance and drive away the Lombards that opposed him. But because 'bright hopes are by their omens oft deceiv'd' he was disappointed in his plan, because it turned out now that it was far worse for him. The towns of Lombardy had foreseen his wicked plan and evil intentions against themselves and had, therefore, hurried to meet him together. Milan, however, when it had received sure information of the headlong advance of its army, did not wait for the other towns, but with Piacenza and captains from the picked troops of Verona, Brescia, Novara and Vercelli, marched out on the first Saturday of June with its *caroccio* and came in high courage to a place suited to themselves between Barrano and Brescia, at the fifteenth milestone from the city, and about the third hour of the day. They then sent towards Como seven hundred men-at-arms to learn from what quarter their most powerful and redoubtable enemy was advancing upon them. When they had gone almost three miles they met three hundred Germans in whose steps Frederick was following with all his army, girded for battle. Without delay enemy rushed upon enemy and with their drawn swords hacked into one another. But when the Emperor's larger force came up, the Lombards unwillingly gave way, for as they wished to find safety by the Milanese *caroccio*, they could not stand fast in face of the persecutor. However, the pressure of the refugees forced them to retire to a place half a mile beyond the *caroccio*. Then the chosen company of the warriors of Milan, which stood in the rear of the line like an impregnable wall, offered prayer to God and His Apostle Peter and to blessed Ambrose, raised their standards and went forward in confidence and high courage to meet Frederick. At the first onslaught, the standard-bearer of Frederick fell to the ground transfixed by a lance and his corpse remained under the feet of the horses. The Emperor himself, appearing in full armour among the others, easily noticeable because of his gleaming arms, was strongly assailed by the Lombards. He fell from his saddle and straightway was lost sight of. With the Lombards pushing against them, the whole German force turned and fled in panic eight miles. A mere handful of so great an army escaped, for some fell by the sword, others were drowned in the Ticino, and the rest were divided among various towns as captives. But the faithless populace of Como which had rashly and senselessly abandoned the unity of the Church and the League of the Lombards, remained on the battlefield almost entirely cut down, either slain by the sword, or led off shamefully into captivity. After the glorious triumph of a longed-for victory the conquering League of the Lombards eagerly gathered together all their booty and in peace they each took possession of what good fortune had given them. Among the spoils of war, besides a great number of arms and horses, were found riches beyond value and the earth's best fruits far beyond the greediest dreams.

Now of the person of the Emperor, whether he had escaped or

lay in death with the others on the battlefield, there was for a long time widespread uncertainty, so much so that his Queen, giving herself up to sadness and mourning, even put on widow's weeds. But while the whole of Italy was of two minds over this matter, he suddenly appeared in Pavia, shorn of his immense store of war-gear and his military forces. It was obvious that in this God was demonstrating the truth He had spoken through Isaiah: 'The eyes of the proud are brought low, and the greatness of strong men is brought down.' Since his cause from the time when he had undertaken the persecution of the Church of God had gone from bad to worse, and though no adversity or difficulty had drawn him back from what he had taken in hand, he was now so buffeted and ground down by the Judge on high, that it seemed to be his humble inclination to establish peace in the Church which he, in his double-dealing, had sought to capture. He thus begged his lord, Pope Alexander, and his brother-Bishops through the more important personages of his Empire. Indeed all the Princes of his Kingdom, both ecclesiastical and secular, who until that time had followed Frederick in his errors, told him that unless he made peace with the Church they would follow him no longer, nor give him any aid. At the same time, the Lord had raised up once more the League of the Lombards against the Germans to such a pitch of courage and vigour that they gained the field at the first onset whenever they joined battle with that uncouth horde and scattered them like wind-blown straw and put them to flight before their faces.

The Emperor sent therefore into the presence of his lord, Pope Alexander, Wichmann, Archbishop of Magdeburg, Christian and Conrad, the bishops elect of Mainz and Worms, and the Protonotary of the Kingdom, Arduin, the most important Princes of his Empire, with full powers to conclude a peace between the Church and the Empire. When they reached Tivoli, they announced to the Pontiff, who was residing at Anagni, the reason of their arrival. They requested safe conduct, were received by two Cardinals and the Captains of Campagna and conducted with all honours into the town of Anagni.

On the next day, while the Pontiff with a great concourse of clerks and nobles was seated in Consistory, the envoys came to the more important Church with a suitable company, and from there went into the presence of the Pontiff. Standing in the middle of the Consistory before him and speaking with the utmost reverence, they said: 'Our lord the Emperor, being most desirous to grant you and the Church of Rome true peace, has sent us with plenary powers to your presence and urgently requests that that agreement of concord and peace, which last year your brothers negotiated with him and which has remained through his fault a dead letter, be now concluded by us and with your consent, under the protection of God, and in every detail. For it is well known and beyond a shadow of doubt that God Almighty has from the first days of the infant Church willed that there should be two powers on earth by which, mainly, the world ought to be ruled, the dignity of the priesthood and the royal power. Unless they support one another in harmony, peace cannot be preserved and the world will be filled with the din of disputes and wars. Let then this hateful disorder come to an end, and the longed-for peace be restored by the two first men of this world to all the churches and to Christendom.'

When this message had been heard in public the kindly Pope with a joyful and calm appearance replied: 'We rejoice at your arrival and the happy tidings that you bring, and for these reasons give thanks to God Almighty. In the visible world there is no message that falls so sweetly upon our ears as the news that the Emperor, your lord, whom we recognize as first amongst the princes of the world, wishes, as you declare, to give us true peace. But if he wishes to give us and the Roman Church full peace, he must grant it also to all our allies, and in particular to the King of Sicily, the Lombards, and to the Emperor in Constantinople, who stood unshakeably with us during the trials of the Church.' The envoys both assented to and praised this speech of the Pontiff and then said: 'We have been instructed by our lord to speak with you and your brethren in secret, so that no disaffected person may come to know of what is to be negotiated and decided between us and you, so that these matters may be kept secret until the boon of peace is concluded in the presence of God. For we know that both on our side and yours there are those who hate peace and are wilfully fomenting discord.'

When these matters had been heard, the whole Consistory withdrew and the Pontiff, with no other companions save his brother Cardinals and the envoys, entered into a conclave. They began seriously to negotiate the terms of the peace, but since the negotiations were arduous and extremely difficult (many of the nobility and the potentates had fallen grievously into schism and disputes had arisen between the Church and the Empire concerning certain

99

articles), they lasted for more than a fortnight. During this period the authority of the holy Fathers, the privileges of the Emperors, the ancient customs and a thousand other matters were brought forward, and over these matters there was long toil and subtle disputation. At length, through the grace of the Holy Spirit, unanimous agreement was reached between the Pontiff and his Cardinals and the envoys on all matters touching the peace of the Church and the Empire. The Lombards' cause remained as it was until there could be a common assembly, since it neither could nor should be finally settled in their absence. And since, as we have just said, peace could not be made except in the actual presence of both the Emperor and the Lombards, it was agreed that the Pontiff, for the sake of so longed-for a peace, should shun no personal discomfort and set out for Lombardy without delay. In the meantime firm guarantees were given by those of the imperial party for all personages of the Church of Rome and their goods, for the Patrimony of St. Peter and the King of Sicily, and all travellers, until the peace was signed.

When these matters had been disposed of and agreed upon, the envoys returned in haste to the Emperor. But Pope Alexander, that he might without delay go to his meeting with the Emperor, set a Vicar over the City of Rome, and with his Cardinals made his way towards the Adriatic. He came to Benevento, and then went through Troia, Santa Maria di Siponto and over Monte Gargano to Vieste, a town by the sea. For there the devoted son of St. Peter, the King of Sicily, had made ready seven galleys for his use, provisioned and armed as both time and circumstances demanded. He had appointed also two of the most important personages of his island, Romuald, Archbishop of Salerno and Roger, Count of Andria, to attend the person of his lord and father, that in their company he might proceed with the greatest honours. To inform the Lombards and the Emperor of his coming, Alexander had sent on ahead from Santa Maria di Siponto six of his brother Cardinals who were to ride to Bologna with his household and those of his brethren.

At that time, the Greek Emperor, Manuel, wishing to bring the Turkish dominions under his rule, invaded them with a great force and advanced almost as far as Konya, the capital of the Sultanate, looting and putting towns and villages to the torch. Then the Sultan, who is the most powerful of the rulers of these people, summoned to his side ten thousand Arabs, more skilled in warfare than all the other peoples of their land, and advanced to meet the Emperor with a great mass of soldiers and archers of his own. The Sultan continually requested him to leave him in peace in his land and to take him into his service. He offered him great and precious gifts in the hope of gaining the Emperor's love and favour, and finally wished humbly to display his loyalty and homage and to enter his service with his soldiers and archers whenever it should be required of him. But the Emperor, highly confident of his strength and power (for the forces which he had with him both on land and sea were both very powerful and very large), spurned the Sultan and told him: 'You will make neither peace nor agreement with me, unless you make over to me and my power the city of Konya.' When he heard this, the Sultan, like the clever and cunning man that he was, pretended to withdraw. But scaling the mountains above the entrance to the pass through which the Emperor had planned to march upon Konya, the Sultan set ambushes for him, to fall upon him unexpectedly and bring him into perilous straits. The Emperor, believing that the Sultan's withdrawal was due more to his fear than to his cleverness or cunning, entered that difficult and narrow pass between those two rugged peaks with too little forethought, nay, rather carelessly and rashly. He had put at the head of his forces the cavalry with the chariots and the most important of the chief men of the state and they all fell into the trap laid for them by their enemies. On both sides a terrible shout was raised and a fearful struggle to death was begun. But since the extreme narrowness of the site allowed the Christians neither escape nor resistance, they were all trapped like a flock of sheep in a fold. To be brief, mercilessly butchered by the savagery of Turks and Arabs, despoiled of great riches of many kinds, only few of that great host survived to be led into captivity. At the rear was found the Emperor, clad in armour and surrounded by a great number of soldiers. As he was being overwhelmed by the swords of the infidels, the Sultan came up and, recognizing him, out of the excessive goodness of his heart (he was bound by his law and feared his Maker), pardoned him and set him free, though he might have exacted full compensation for the wrong that the Emperor had done him. He also thought it a worthy thing to restore to the Emperor the crown and the most precious Cross which had been captured, with many gifts of many kinds. Finally, he made peace with him there and then, and in this way they departed from each other.

In the meantime, when the news was brought to that laughable antipope of Viterbo, who, an object of ridicule, was forever going from bad to worse, that friendly negotiations were going on for peace and harmony between the Pope and the Emperor without him, and when he learnt without any possibility of error that a firm pledge of safety had been given to all who used the roads, he and his partisans were as deeply grieved as if his heart had been broken.

Before he left Anagni, Pope Alexander sent Hu., Cardinal Bishop of Ostia and R., Cardinal of St. George, ahead to the imperial court, to obtain from the Emperor openly and under oath the safe conduct which the Archbishop of Magdeburg and his fellow envoys had promised. They went through Tuscany and came to Lombardy and in the vicinity of Modena found the Emperor in quite a peaceful mood. He greeted them with a smile and with respect and honoured them with great ceremony. And so, in the presence of many Bishops and Princes and of the envoys themselves he had C., the son of the Markgrave of Monferrato, swear upon his soul on the Gospels the same safe conduct which the envoys had granted at Anagni. Furthermore, as a clearer instance of the goodwill he felt towards the peace, he had all the Princes of Germany in his company corroborate the same safe conduct by oath.

In those days, Cremona, looking back, and without any serious cause, basely broke trust, shamelessly withdrew from the League of the cities, and not without great scandal went over to the Emperor. For this reason it justly incurred the wrath of the Church and the hatred and enmity of the other Lombard cities. Tortona also did the same thing not long after, and is to be blamed for it, and so involved itself insolently in the same scaldal. When the Pope heard this news at Vieste he was very surprised, but remained certain of the firmness of the other cities.

After a great storm at sea had kept him at Vieste in spite of his plans and against his will, all of a sudden the long-awaited south wind blew up and straightway and swiftly brought up the ships that were to carry the Pope. He himself arose about midnight on the first day of Lent and very early, after Mass and receiving the ashes, cheerfully set out into the deep with eleven galleys and two other ships to carry provisions and the white horses. It was a delightful thing to see that bright fleet, making its wake through the wide sea, its sails pulling well and the wind propitious. But about midday the south wind died away entirely and the north wind sprang up in its place and there and then the sea was heaped up into a confusion of waves.

All were afraid. The Pope did not feel himself at all safe, since the great strength of the squalls gave much cause for alarm. Ten of the galleys bearing the Pope and his Cardinals struggled, the oarsmen bending to their oars, towards the nearest islands, and at length aided by the prayers of the holy Apostles Peter and Paul they came safely, thank God! about nightfall to the island of Pelagosa. But the ships that bore the white horses and the rearmost galley returned to Vieste, because they were not able to struggle against the wind and follow the other vessels. The Pontiff, worn out by his fasting and the buffetting from the storm-tossed sea, willingly disembarked, and when the board was laid, partook of a large and cheerful dinner. But after some interval of time, when they were all at rest, unexpectedly the south wind they were looking for smiled upon the sailors, and urged them to continue their journey. There was fierce joy in the hearts of all, sails were most quickly spread, and every man remained watchfully ready to carry out his duty in the darkness of the night itself. The galley of the Supreme Pontiff was the swiftest, and went first, showing a great light. They all sailed on through the night and on the next day they celebrated Mass and with great joy and gladness partook of dinner about midday on the island of Lissa. Sailing thence through the other islands of Dalmatia, they came on the following Sunday, before sunrise, to the town of Zadar which is situated where the Kingdom of Hungary comes down to the sea. With the help of St. Peter, the ships carried the Supreme Pontiff there in good health and high spirits with his brethren, M., Bishop of Praeneste; I., Cardinal Priest of the title of Santa Anastasia; B., Cardinal Priest of the title of Santa Pudentiana; C. and U., the Cardinal Deacons of the titles of St. Adrian and of St. Eustachius; Romuald, Archbishop of Salerno and the illustrious Count Roger. And since no Roman Pontiff had ever visited the town, joy and rejoicing beyond words was felt by both clergy and people of the locality at the recent arrival of Pope Alexander. They gave praise to and blessed God, Who in these latter times had deigned to visit His church of Zadar in the person of His servant Alexander, the successor of St. Peter. And so when a white horse had been made ready for him in the Roman way, they led him in procession through the town to the more important of the churches, to Santa Anastasia, in which the virgin martyr herself lies buried in honour, with endless songs and chants of praise ringing about him in their Slavonic tongue. After a four days' stay he left Zadar and, making a pleasant voyage through the islands of the Slavs and past the small sea-coast towns of Istria, he came with glad heart to the monastery of St. Nicholas, situated at the sea-coast on the Lido.

And so on 24 March of the eighteenth year of his pontificate, in the tenth indiction, Pope Alexander entered Venice for the first time in great pomp and ceremony. He was met by the Doge, by the Patriarch, the Bishops, the nobility, and the clergy in a varied and great fleet of boats. When he had taken up residence in the Palace of the Patriarch on the Rialto, the aforesaid Archbishop of Magdeburg with the Bishop elect of Worms and the Protonotary came to him with the following message: 'Our Lord the Emperor is ready with glad heart to conclude all those matters that through our mediation have been negotiated and drafted; but he will not meet you in Bologna which is very suspect to his Princes. For this reason we humbly beg your clemency that you would be so good as to choose another city that is pleasing both to him and to you, either Ravenna or Venice.' Without delay the Pontiff answered him firmly: 'It has been a long time since through the mediation of our brethren, U., Cardinal Bishop of Ostia and Cardinal Deacon R. and the Lombards, the Emperor agreed that we should come together, he in Imola and we in Bologna; and so we neither can nor ought to change that place without the consent of the Lombards or the advice of our brethren who in the suburbs of the latter town are awaiting our arrival. If what of his own accord he formerly granted is now displeasing to him, he ought to put aside all excuses and lay the blame at his own door and not at ours. But, so that the boon of the peace which is coming into being may be brought by the aid of God all the more quickly to its desired completion, we shall take pains to come without delay to Ferrara, to be able to hold deliberation with our absent brethren and the rulers of Lombardy and to make a full choice as to what ought to be done and as to what is most agreeable to both parties.' Since this reply gave great pleasure to the envoys, he bade by Apostolic letter all Bishops and the Rectors of the towns of Lombardy to assemble under divine Protection on Passion Sunday in that very town.

But in the meantime, since great crowds were pressing in upon him and a great concourse of notables from the neighbouring towns was gathering in his presence, to hear and see him as an angel sent from God, he considered it fitting that on the following Sunday, *Laetare*, he should celebrate the solemn rites of the Mass in the

Cathedral of St. Mark. Clad in the sacred vestments and bearing, as is customary for that day, the Golden Rose, he advanced with great devotion in procession to the altar with his Bishops and Cardinals. After the reading of the Gospel, he preached in accordance with his duty as a shepherd of the flock to the people of God which had assembled from every district and when the rites of the Mass had come to an end, he presented the Rose he bore to the Doge of Venice as a token of the favour of the Apostolic See towards him.

During the same week, with a bright fleet of galleys, a most delightful sight indeed, he left Venice, and making his way up through the mouth of the Po, came with great pomp and ceremony to his own city of Ferrara. On the next day the chief personages from each side gathered before the Pontiff. Their names are given below. On the side of the Lombards were the Patriarch of Aquileia, the Archbishops of Milan and Ravenna, and the Bishops of their provinces, the Rectors of the towns with their Markgraves and Counts, the Archbishop of Salerno and Roger, Count of Andria. On the side of the Emperor were the Archbishops of Mainz, Cologne, Trier, Besançon, Magdeburg, and Salzburg, with some of their suffragans; there was also the Bishop elect of Worms and Arduin, the Protonotary. When they were all assembled, a great dispute arose between the parties about a place where the Pope could presently meet the Emperor in security. The Lombards asked for Bologna, or Piacenza, or Ferrara, or Padua; while the Imperial princes were for Pavia, or Ravenna, or Venice. The Pope, with the envoys of the King of Sicily, chose Venice because the following conditions could be observed there: each side could go to Venice with light heart if the Doge and people of Venice were to guarantee on oath that until the peace was finally concluded, they would on no account allow the Emperor to enter Venice without the agreement of the Pope, and that they would put no impediment in the way of those who were either going to or coming from the city. This, on the instruction of the Pontiff, was carried out.

He left Ferrara with his Bishops and Cardinals on the 25 April, and came without delay to Venice, and both sides followed him quickly.

When then the Princes and the Lombards were arranged in order in the presence of the Pontiff, negotiations were begun on the restoration of peace between them. But mainly because of the king's rights (*regalia*) and because of fiefs, the differences between the parties were very great, and because peace for the Church ought not to be made without peace for those who had stood stoutly by it against the Empire, the negotiations, with many adjournments, went on until the Octave of the Apostles Peter and Paul. On that day the peace of the Church, in that form which had been agreed to with the consent of the parties and confirmed in writing, was confirmed also by the assent of the Emperor with the unanimous agreement of the Princes who were present. The peace with the King of Sicily which was to run from the following 1 August for fifteen years was adopted in the same way. On these matters charters were drawn up by agreement on both sides and were accepted with good will by each of the parties.

When all this had been done, the Pontiff gave, at the insistence of the Princes, permission for the Emperor to come to Chioggia, so that in that town, only a short distance away from the Pontiff, the negotiations of the Cardinals and Princes who had brought almost to finality the terms of the Peace and of the Truces, on their coming before him, might by the imperial authority and the help of God gain full effect and an unalterable firmness. The Emperor came thither and the Cardinals and Princes both assembled in his presence, and announced all they had done with his agreement. When he had heard everything that had been done and fully understood it, though he was beset and warned by those who hated peace, because the Princes before him manfully withstood him to his face he ratified and promised to confirm of his own accord everything that had been negotiated and inscribed in the presence of the Pope. And so in the hearing of the Cardinals and Princes he instructed Count Dedo, son of the Markgrave Conrad, to swear in public upon his soul before the Pope and the envoys of the King of Sicily and of the Lombards in this fashion: 'I, Count Dedo, swear that my Lord the Emperor has instructed me to swear upon my soul the oath which I am now about to utter, and that after he gave me this instruction he did not revoke it. And I, on the instructions of the Emperor, swear upon his soul that as soon as he comes to Venice, he, putting aside all questions and controversies, will swear upon his soul that he will with good will keep the Peace of the Church as it has been arranged by the negotiators and written down, the Fifteen Year Peace with the King of Sicily, as it has been written down, as well as the Truce with the Lombards, as was arranged by negotiators from both sides, and under the written terms that are in the possession of those nego-

106

tiators. His Princes also shall swear the selfsame oath.' He gave a similar instruction to his Chamberlain Sigilboth: 'I, Sigilboth, swear that when my Lord the Emperor comes to Venice, he will take upon his soul an oath concerning the Peace of the Church and of the King of Sicily and of the Truce of the Lombards, and shall have his Princes swear likewise.'

And so when these matters had been brought to completion in this way, the Pontiff released the Doge and the people of Venice from the oath which bound them, and instructed them to escort the Lord Emperor with due ceremony into their city. The Doge hastened to fulfil this instruction, and with due honours and ceremony brought the Emperor to the monastery of St. Nicholas on the Lido in six galleys which he had made ready. On the following day on the Vigil of St. James, when morning was at its height, the Pope sent to the Emperor the Bishops of Ostia, Porto and Praeneste, Hu., G., and M., with I., Cardinal Priest of the title of Santa Anastasia; T., Cardinal Priest of the title of Santa Vitalia; P., Cardinal Priest of the title of Santa Susanna, and I., Cardinal Deacon of the title of St. Mary in Cosmidin. They came into the presence of the Emperor, and after he had renounced the Schism of Octavian, Guy of Crema, and John of Strumi, and promised obedience to the venerable Pope Alexander as to the first person in Christendom and to his successors who would enter on their office according to the canons, they absolved him from the sentence of excommunication that had been passed upon him and made him once more part of the unity of the Catholic Church. Some of the more important Princes of his Empire made the same renunciation according to the ancient custom of the Church. Thereupon the Emperor, like the orthodox prince that he now was, approached the presence of the same Pontiff, who was enthroned with his Archbishops, Bishops, and Cardinals before the doors of St. Mark's; and in the sight of all who awaited the benefit of the peace he put off his cloak and bowed down to the ground, and after kissing the Pope's feet just as if they were those of the first of the Apostles, in verity he most devoutly administered the kiss of peace to him. Then were all filled with great joy, and from the excess of their gladness the sound of their chanting of the *Te Deum* rose up to the skies. But the august monarch, taking the Pontiff by his right hand, and amid chants and hymns of praise led him to the choir of the church, and there reverently received with bowed head the blessing from his hand.

On the next day, the feast of St. James the Apostle, the Pope returned to the same church, and being about to celebrate the rites of the Mass with a joyous procession of Patriarchs, Cardinals, Bishops, Priests, and Deacons and the other orders of the Church, he drew near to the altar. The Emperor took his place in the choir, and the German clergy began in clear voices to chant the Introit of the Mass, and with all jubilation carried out the whole chanting of the service. After the Gospel and the homily, the Emperor once again, together with his Princes, bowed down in a most devout fashion, opened his treasures and, after kissing Alexander's feet, made him an offering of gold. When the Mass had been celebrated, Frederick took the Pontiff by the right hand and conducted him outside to his white horse and held his stirrup with a strong grip. But when he took the reins and made as if to carry out the duties of a marshal, the Pope accepted in his loving manner the intention for the deed, since the journey to the sea seemed to him to be rather long.

On the following day, about the ninth hour, the Emperor in filial affection paid a visit to the Pontiff with a small company. With impetuous heart he sought him out even so far as his private room, where Alexander was seated in familiar conversation with his Bishops and Cardinals. For a long time they expressed their good wishes for each other, and after an affectionate conversation, in which mild pleasantries, which could do no harm to their dignity, were mixed with matters of greater moment, the august Emperor, having asked for and obtained permission, returned with light heart to his lodgings.

On the first day of August, the envoys of the King of Sicily and the Rectors of the towns of Lombardy were summoned, and with the Pope and the Emperor they entered into a Consistory. Then the Emperor rising in the presence of the Pope, in the hearing of them all bade Count Henry of Dietz to swear upon his soul that he would keep with a good heart peace between the Church and the Empire, and with the King of Sicily for fifteen years, and the Truce with the Lombards from the first day of August for six years, just as the negotiators from both sides had agreed to and written down. And furthermore he bade those Princes who were present likewise to swear and to maintain with goodwill the same peace and the truces. Quickly the Count took his oath upon the holy book of Gospels as the Emperor had bade him to, and then turned and said to him:

'Thus may God and these holy Gospels give you aid.' One by one the princes followed him; the Archbishops Christian of Mainz; Philip of Cologne; Wichmann of Magdeburg; Arnold of Trier; D. of Utrecht; Conrad, the Bishop elect of Worms; Arduin, Protonotary of the Imperial Court; C. the former Bishop of Mantua; Godfrey, the Chancellor, and Count C. 'I swear,' they said, 'upon my soul and upon these holy Gospels that I will keep with good faith and without fraud the peace between the Church and the Empire, and for fifteen years with the King of Sicily, and a truce for six years with the Lombards, as has been decided and written down by the negotiators of each side. So help me God and these holy Gospels.' The Archbishop of Salerno, Romuald, and Roger, Count of Andria swore the same oath on behalf of the King of Sicily. On behalf of the Lombards those who were present took the oath: Gerardo Pistis and the Consul Roger Marcellin, for Milan; Guglielmo Leccacorvo, for Piacenza; Alberto di Cambara, for Brescia; Alberto Albertone, for Bergamo; Cotto, the Consul, for Verona; Vetulo, for Parma; Artemano, for Reggio; Pinamonte, the podestà, for Bologna; Guglielmo Guibuini for Novara; Uberto di Fuoro, for Alessandria; the podestà Tessulino, for Padua; and Ezzolino, for Vincenza.

When the Emperor had been absolved, the usurpers and schismatics who had been his followers returned in droves to the bosom of their mother the Church. They humbly begged for absolution and repudiated and anathematized on the holy Gospels every heresy that had raised itself against the holy Church of Rome, and in particular the heresy and schism of Octavian, Guy of Crema and John of Struma. They declared their orders void, and promised to be faithful and obedient to their lord, Pope Alexander, and to his Catholic successors. Thus they were reconciled and reunited to the wholeness of the Catholic faith. It is our opinion that the more important of them ought to be named: Christian of Mainz, Philip of Cologne, Wichmann of Magdeburg, the Bishops of Trier and Utrecht, the Bishop elect of Worms, the Bishops of Augsburg, Basel, Strassburg, Halbertstadt, Pavia, Piacenza, Cremona, Brescia, Novara, Acqui, C. of Mantua, Bagnorea, Pesaro, and Fano, one V., who had been promoted deacon by Guy of Crema, a former Abbot of Cluny and the usurper of St. Peter in Celo Aureo, and his neighbour the usurper of St. Saviour. It is beyond our powers to make a list of the great number of other schismatics who returned to their senses.

In the same period, on 15 August in the Church of St. Mark

at Venice Pope Alexander with his Archbishops, Bishops, and other prelates of the churches of Italy and Germany held a Synod, in which the Emperor himself had his throne at the side of the Pope. During this Synod the peace between the Church and the Empire and with the King of Sicily and the Truce with the Lombards which had been previously arranged, were once again ratified and confirmed by the declaration of all present. But to give it an even greater firmness, the Pope decreed a sentence of excommunication as follows: that whoever should break the Peace or the Truce, and did not make satisfaction within forty days of having been required to and admonished, should incur the same sentence and be without excuse for this action. Those schismatics who had not yet come to their senses, he bound with a sentence of excommunication until they did satisfaction.

In those days Cavalcante, Count of Bertinoro died childless at Venice. For the forgiveness of his sins and those of his parents, he bequeathed the castle of Bertinoro, which is also known as Susubio, and all its territory, since it had in olden times belonged to St. Peter, to the holy Church of Rome for her own possession, and in confirmation of the legacy, he caused the document for Pope Alexander and his successors to be made public. Wherefore, to receive the investiture of the castle itself which is the chief point and the seat of the County, the Pontiff sent there without delay the Cardinal Deacon R., the Subdeacon R., and Peter Sarracenus, his steward, through whom he received by investiture the possession of that County into the power and government of the Apostolic See and held it.

To their Lord and Father, the Venerable Alexander, by the grace of God the Supreme Pontiff and Pope of the Holy See of Rome and of the Catholic Church, we, Christian, Archbishop of Mainz; Philip, Archbishop of Cologne; Wichmann, Archbishop of Magdeburg; Arnold, Archbishop of Trier; Conrad, Bishop elect of Worms; Godfrey, Chancellor; Wortwin, Protonotary; Florentinus, Count of Holland; T., Markgrave of Lusatia, and his brother Dedo; Henry, Count of Dietz; and Rupert, Count of Durna, give our service of filial devotion with due obedience and subjection.

The advantages which flow to the whole world from the peace that has been made between the Church and the Empire and those innumerable evils which are thereby avoided are clear for all to see. For as the world is directed towards safety and peace by the harmonious providence of each power, so through their division was it torn away from the proper condition of rectitude. Let therefore the earth rejoice that it has been bedewed by the fall of so desirable a dew, made fertile by the downpour of so pleasant a rain, by which the thirst of the faithful is assuaged and the scandal of every dispute and the fire of every scandal extinguished. Most Holy Father, we rejoice in so rich a harvest of the fruits of your agreement, the most sacred Peace between the Church and the Empire, settled by the negotiators of each side and published in an agreed text, the Peace which has been concluded for fifteen years with the King of Sicily and the Truce with the Lombards which is to last for six years from the first day of August next, exactly according to the terms arranged by the negotiators, confirmed by our oaths, and published in an agreed text; this text, moreover, is confirmed by the signatures of the negotiators of either side and authenticated with their seals. These treaties we affirm by the eagerness and firmness of our assent. We consider them to be both ratified and inviolable and we will take care to have them observed. And in order that this page which contains our agreement may remain unimpaired and unaltered for the centuries to come, we have ordered our own signatures and our own seals to be affixed to it.

+Christian, Archbishop of the See of Mainz
+Philip, Archbishop of Cologne, and Archchancellor of Italy
+Conrad, Bishop elect of Worms
+Godfrey, Chancellor of the Imperial Palace
+Wortwin, Protonotary

To the revered father in Christ, the Lord Pope Alexander, Supreme and Universal Pontiff of the Roman Church, Frederick, by the Grace of God, Emperor of the Romans and ever August, gives due obedience and filial devotion.

Since the imperial majesty has been ordered on earth by the King of Kings so that by its operation the whole world may rejoice at the increase of peace, we, whom God has placed on the throne of the Roman Empire, will and shall embrace it more fervently and preserve it more eagerly. It is for this reason that we confirm the Peace made between the Church and the Empire according to the terms negotiated and set out by our Princes and the Cardinals of the Church of Rome and sealed with the seals of our Princes, and according to the text of the instrument which we, through out delegates, have sworn to. We wish it to remain in force for succeeding generations. Thus hereafter we shall observe its terms closely and cause it, as much as lies in our power, by the mercy of God, to be observed.

Given at Venice, in the Palace of the Doge, on the 17th day of September, in the tenth indiction.

At this time, on the Vigil of the Feast of the Apostle St. Matthew, Pope Alexander, came to the end of the eighteenth year of his pontificate.

The nineteenth year of the pontificate begins.

When the peace had been ratified in the manner which I have described, all returned with joy in their hearts to their own lands. At the end of a few days, some of the nobles of Treviso withdrew from the Lombard League and approached the presence of the Emperor. With him they spoke for a long time in private about secret matters and exchanged certain oaths. For this reason they became hateful and objects of great suspicion to the Lombards. When they returned to their own estates, the people of Treviso rose against them, and called them, with dreadful cries, perjurers and odious men, traitors to their own country and worthy of a most shameful death. In short, to bring themselves out of the peril of death, there and then they swore on the book of the Gospels, that they would reveal in their entirety to the rulers of the Lombards their secret conversations with the Emperor and the form of their oaths. Moreover, they gave their sons as hostages and sufficient pledges that they would stand firmly by the instructions of the Rectors in these matters. The noblemen were taken aside. They revealed by a public charter to the Rectors of the Lombards their oaths and secret conversations with the Emperor. When their treason and its malice was revealed and made manifest, the Lombard League punished the noblemen severly according to their deserts, and thereafter watched all the more carefully for the plots of their cunning enemy, and strengthened themselves all the more.

While matters stood thus, the Emperor wanted to depart from Venice and sought audience with the Supreme Pontiff in the palace of the Patriarch where he was residing, in order to obtain his permission to do so. When all others had left the court, he conferred with the Pope about those matters which still remained outstanding for the conclusion of the peace. Only the Bishops and Cardinals and the imperial Princes were in attendance upon them. Then the Pontiff requested the Emperor to have restored to him the *regalia* of St. Peter and the possessions of the Holy Roman Church, as the Cardinals and Princes who acted as negotiators had agreed and affirmed at Anagni. The Emperor in reply said: 'I shall restore immediately the *regalia* of St. Peter and the other possessions of the Roman Church, except the lands of the Countess Matilda and of the

Count of Bertinoro. Because these latter lands seem to me to belong to the rights of the Empire, choose three of our Princes, and we shall choose the same number from your Cardinals, to negotiate about these matters, and each side shall stand irrevocably by their decision.' Although this was something serious and difficult for the Pontiff, since in the Treaty of Peace the restoration of the territory of the Countess Matilda had been expressly mentioned and sworn to and since the Castle of Bertinoro, as we have described, was in his possession, yet not to disturb the peace of the Church on these pretexts, he finally gave assent to the Emperor's wish, and straight-away chose Christian, Archbishop of Mainz; Conrad, Bishop elect of Worms; and Arduin, the Protonotary, who were in attendance, for that purpose, while the Emperor chose the Cardinal Bishops of Ostia and Porto and the Cardinal Deacon James, in his turn. For the restoration of the *regalia* and the other possessions of the Church, the Emperor there and then appointed Mainz, bidding him to complete the restoration in its entirety within three months if he wished to remain in his favour.

When these matters had been arranged and settled amicably, the august Emperor went down on his knees before the Pontiff, kissed his feet, and received from him and all the Cardinals the kiss of peace. With this farewell he retired towards Ravenna and Cesena. After his departure and about the middle of October the Pontiff requested four galleys from the Doge of Venice, and having sent on ahead the greater number of his brethren by the coast road through Pentapolis along the sea coast, he once more set out into the deep under the protection of God. Returning by the same route as he had come, he reached Santa Maria di Siponto on 29 October in good health, thanks to the prayers of the holy Apostles Peter and Paul. From that port he made a progress through Troia, Benevento, and San Germano with great pomp and ceremony and arrived safe and sound at the city of Anagni which was so greatly devoted to him on 14 December, a fact for which we give thanks to God.

At the Pope's peaceful and so long looked-for return there was great rejoicing in the city of Rome and in the whole of its territories, and among those who blessed and praised the Lord there was joy in every heart, for He had, through the unwearied prayers and toil of the keeper of the keys of St. Peter, vouchsafed the return of peace and harmony between Church and Empire. In particular, some of that great horde of schismatics who had usurped various offices, returned of their own accord to their obedience to Pope Alexander, and others abandoned their churches to Catholics and fled in shame and confusion to their own families. The chief of their conventicle, when the news went abroad that the Emperor had gone in and kissed the feet of Pope Alexander, was troubled to the depths of his being, and as a result of the terror that arose in him on perceiving that he was alone, so great a fear and trembling came upon him that he left Viterbo in secret and, like an outlaw, he fled in vain to Monte Albano, to seek the flimsy protection of John, the lord of that castle. When he heard this, the Emperor displayed great sorrow. Seeking to excuse his own conduct, he withdrew his protection from John and placed him under the ban of the Empire, unless he quickly returned to his obedience to Pope Alexander.

We have not thought it necessary to pass over in silence the fact that as soon as he reached Cesena, the Emperor following the advice of evil men, marched on Bertinoro and summoned the aforementioned envoys to him, R., the Cardinal Deacon of St. George; R., the Subdeacon for the Apostolic See; and the Pope's steward, P. He demanded of them at once the possession of the castle with all its appurtenances. The envoys gave him the kind and gentle answer that without the permission and instruction of their lord the Roman Pontiff they neither could nor would do such a thing. He straightway brushed aside their objections and, surrounding them with his army, expelled them from the castle and took that impregnable fortress without any struggle or battle. The men of that locality had to swear fealty to himself and his son. Nor should this turn of events surprise us, since between the Bulgari and the Mainardi, who were the braver troops of that place, there had arisen contentions and the latter had granted their favour to the Emperor. When news of this came to the ears of the Pontiff, he sent some of the more important personages of the Church to speak with the Emperor in fatherly fashion and, with solicitude and urgency, begged him to restore in peace the possession of that castle to himself and to holy Mother Church. But the Emperor, persisting with the strength of his will, refused utterly to make restitution. Though this event caused great pain and distress to the Pope and the Church, it was considered preferable to suffer and pretend it had not happened unless this wrong might be an occasion of bringing to an end the peace that had just been concluded and the harmony which was of the greatest benefit both to Church and to Empire. The Pope would not make charges to counter the accusations of the Emperor, but preferred to wait until the Lord softened the heart of the Emperor and he of his own accord restored to the Church what was rightfully her own.

Here follows the text of the Privilege of the King of Hungary, who gave to the Church of Hungary her liberty out of his respect for the Church of Rome and of the Lord Pope Alexander.

Bela, by the grace of God, King of Hungary, Dalmatia, Croatia, and Rama, to the Archbishops by the same grace, Luke of Esztergom and Cosmas of Kalocsa, and all their suffragans, and to all our officials and to all ecclesiastics who are found in these Archbishoprics, whether now or hereafter for ever.

It is clearly right and entirely conformable to reason, and it is approved by the testimonies of the Holy Scriptures, that they who merit to attain to the summit of royal glory at the hands of the everlasting King, are obliged to attend to those matters which are recognized as being in any way for the advancement of the Church and Christendom. Therefore, persuaded by right reason and by the even greater weight and attention to be attached by the most salutary exhortations of M. the revered Cardinal Deacon of the holy Roman Church, and wishing to be able also to imitate in every way possible the devotion of our Father, King Geza of revered memory, which he had been zealous to display towards the most holy Roman Church and towards our most Holy Father Alexander, the Supreme Pontiff, we confirm and decree that during the course of our reign and those of our successors there is to remain in force and inviolate the Concordat about the deposition and translation of Bishops. This concordat as is well known, our father granted in his own name and those of his successors to Pope Alexander and his successors. The Concordat affirmed that without the advice of the papal authorities the royal power would neither carry out nor permit to be carried out the deposition or translation of Bishops. Moreover, abandoning the customary right that has been held by our predecessors during times past, we decree that for us and our successors this decree will have a validity of unshakable power. On the death of a Bishop we shall not put lay vicars in charge of the episcopal properties, nor allow anyone else to do so, but only honest clerks who will take in moderate fashion revenues from the possessions of the church for the necessities but not for the pleasures of life. These clerks will be required to care for all the other revenues in good faith and without fraud so that the churches and the dwelling of bishops or canons may be restored, and the poor, widows, and orphans be maintained. But neither we nor our successors shall ever take anything of these revenues for our own use unless, which God forbid, the King's enemies enter the territories of his kingdom with a powerful force or unless any other emergency or extreme urgency so demands. Even on these occasions we shall do nothing without the advice of the Bishops. We add, moreover, and decree with unshakable force both for ourselves and for our successors that it is to be observed forever that royal officers or abbots are not to be removed from their offices or abbeys or benefices. In this we renounce on our own behalf and on behalf of our successors our ancient custom, except it should happen by unfortunate mischance that they are convicted of a definite crime against the canons or make public confession of their crime. And, Cosmas, Archbishop of Kalocsa, and all the Bishops, Bishops elect, King's Officers and Abbots, considering the bounty and the liberty that we have granted out of respect for St. Peter, for our most holy Father, Pope Alexander, and for the revered M. Cardinal Deacon and envoy of the Apostolic See, have abandoned entirely into the hands of the aforementioned Cardinal the wicked custom which has been practised, in opposition to the canons, of appointing and removing from offices and other honours and in deposing from ecclesiastical benefices. Wherefore with the unanimous agreement and the willing assent of them all, we decree, and establish as valid and inviolate for ever the present Privilege, that none of the Archbishops, Bishops, Bishops elect, Officers or Abbots, have hereafter permission to remove Officers from their offices or to deprive other ecclesiastical persons of their dignities or ecclesiastical benefices, unless they are convicted acording to the canons of some crime or make confession of it. Let all these matters be known as established and ratified with the advice of the glorious Queen, our mother, of the Archbishops and all the Bishops, the Bishops elect, the King's officers, the Abbots and all the Counts, Chiefs and other Princes.

Done in the city of W., in the year 1169.

In the meanwhile, all the clergy and people of the City of Rome, when they saw the Emperor Frederick under divine inspiration kneeling at the feet of Pope Alexander and the evil of the schism extinguished by the power of God, considered that they had suffered grave loss in matters both spiritual and temporal by reason of the Pontiff's long absence. Therefore, unanimously and happily they decided to recall him to the See of St. Peter. They sent therefore to the Pope at Anagni seven men drawn from the better sort of Roman citizens with letters from the clergy, the Senate and the people, suppliantly begging him to deign to return to his own City and to the people especially entrusted to him and take care of them. The Pope, though their humble and devout invitation gave him and his brother Bishops great pleasure, recalled to mind the past invitation of the same clergy and people to return from countries beyond the Alps, and remembered how many injustices and insults they had heaped on him and his brother Bishops after a short space of time. Not unnaturally, he hesitated to believe in their fine promises and in their pledges of safe conduct and to return to that City which, as is well known, contains many disturbers of the peace. Therefore, with the consent of both sides, Hubert, Cardinal Bishop of Ostia; I., Cardinal Priest of the title of SS. John and Paul; and U., Cardinal Deacon of Sant' Angelo returned to the City, to arrange with the Senate and people the form of the guarantees and the peace which should be pleasing to the Pope and to his brother Bishops. Though the negotiations over these matters were long, at length, by the prayers of the holy Apostles Peter and Paul it was decided on the advice and vote of all the people of Rome that the Senators, who are accustomed to do so, would pay fealty and homage to the Pope and that they would freely restore to his possession and power the Basilica of St. Peter and the *regalia*, which had been seized by them, and that they would keep without fail peace and security for the Pope, his fellow Bishops and their possessions and for all those who approached them or departed from them. When all this had been concluded, the Senate came with these Cardinals and certain other gentlemen into the Pope's presence. They were kindly received at the kissing of the feet and of the cheek, and they, with their hands on the book of the Gospels, swore in public an oath to keep everything that had been decided by the people.

When all these matters had been concluded with the Lord's aid in due form, all rejoiced greatly and thereafter the Pope and his brother Bishops quickly girded themselves for their return to the City. On the next day, the feast of the Pope St. Gregory, before *Laetare* Sunday, he left Tusculum after Mass on his journey to the City, not without much pomp and ceremony. The Roman clergy had gone far out of the City to meet him with banners and crosses. No-one could recollect this had ever been done for a Roman Pontiff. The Senators and Magistrates went with them with strident trumpets, the nobles with their men-at-arms in fitting livery, and the populace on foot, with olive branches, shouting the accustomed *Laudes* for the Pontiff. When he saw the eyes of them all turned toward him as to Jesus Christ, whose Vice-regent on earth he was, his white palfrey could scarcely move forward because of the pressure of the throng which was applying their lips to its footprints. The right hand of its rider grew heavy with the toil of bestowing blessings. With so great and so solemn rejoicing then the Pontiff of the Romans went forward as necessity allowed and arrived, about the ninth hour in extreme weariness, at the Lateran Gate. From there he was conducted to and received in the patriarchal Basilica of the Lateran with all ceremony and with pomp that is beyond the power of tongue to describe. With repeated bursts of praise the Pope went to the altar of the Holy Saviour as Rome's true and good shepherd, the orthodox successor of St. Peter. After bestowing his blessings on the people, he entered his palace, where, after all the Cardinals had returned to their titular churches, he rested for a while from the fatigues of the journey before partaking of food.

On the following day, he went out to a Consistory and received a large crowd of people, both lay and clerical, which kissed his feet according to custom. Afterwards, on *Laetare* Sunday, he went to the church of the Holy Cross, and on Passion Sunday to St. Peter's, carrying out the duties of his office at the accustomed stations of the City. On Easter Sunday, he solemnly took possession of his Kingdom.

Index

There are no entries for Pope Alexander III (Roland Bandinelli) and Emperor Frederick I (Barbarossa) because their names occur on almost every page.